Enter Our World

C.V. Designs

Copyright

R.U. Tokin and C.V. Designs

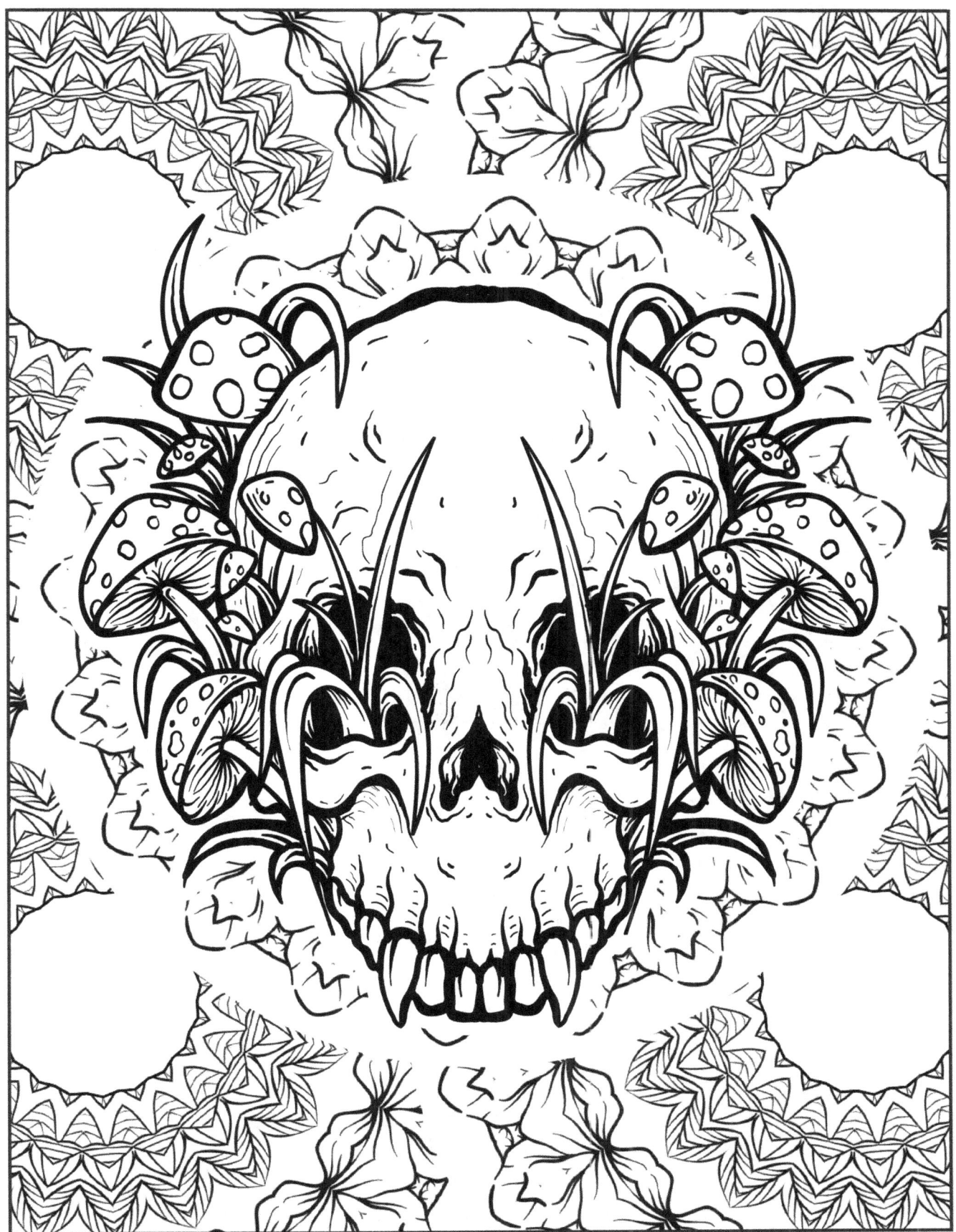

Copyright

R.U. Tokin and C.V. Designs

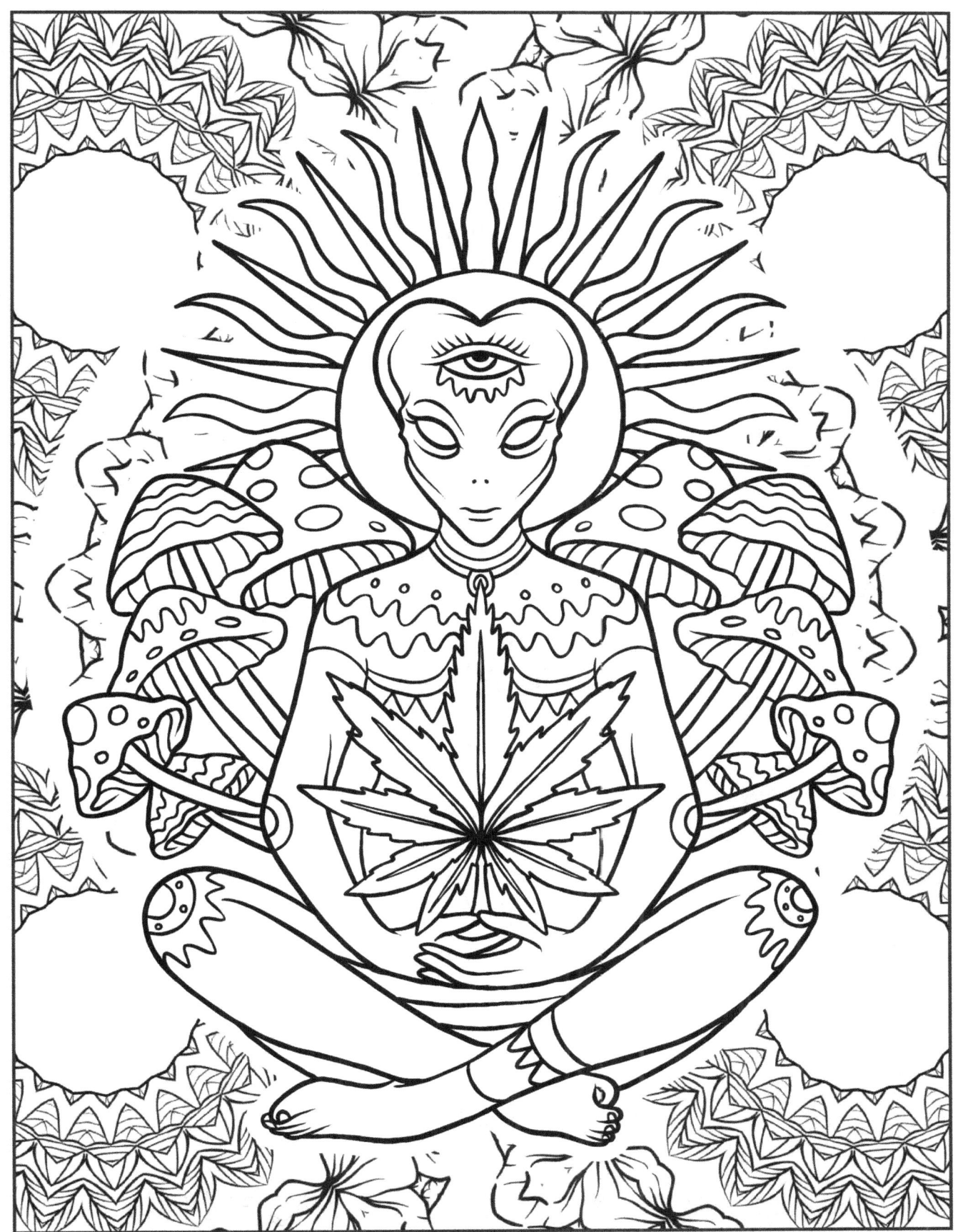

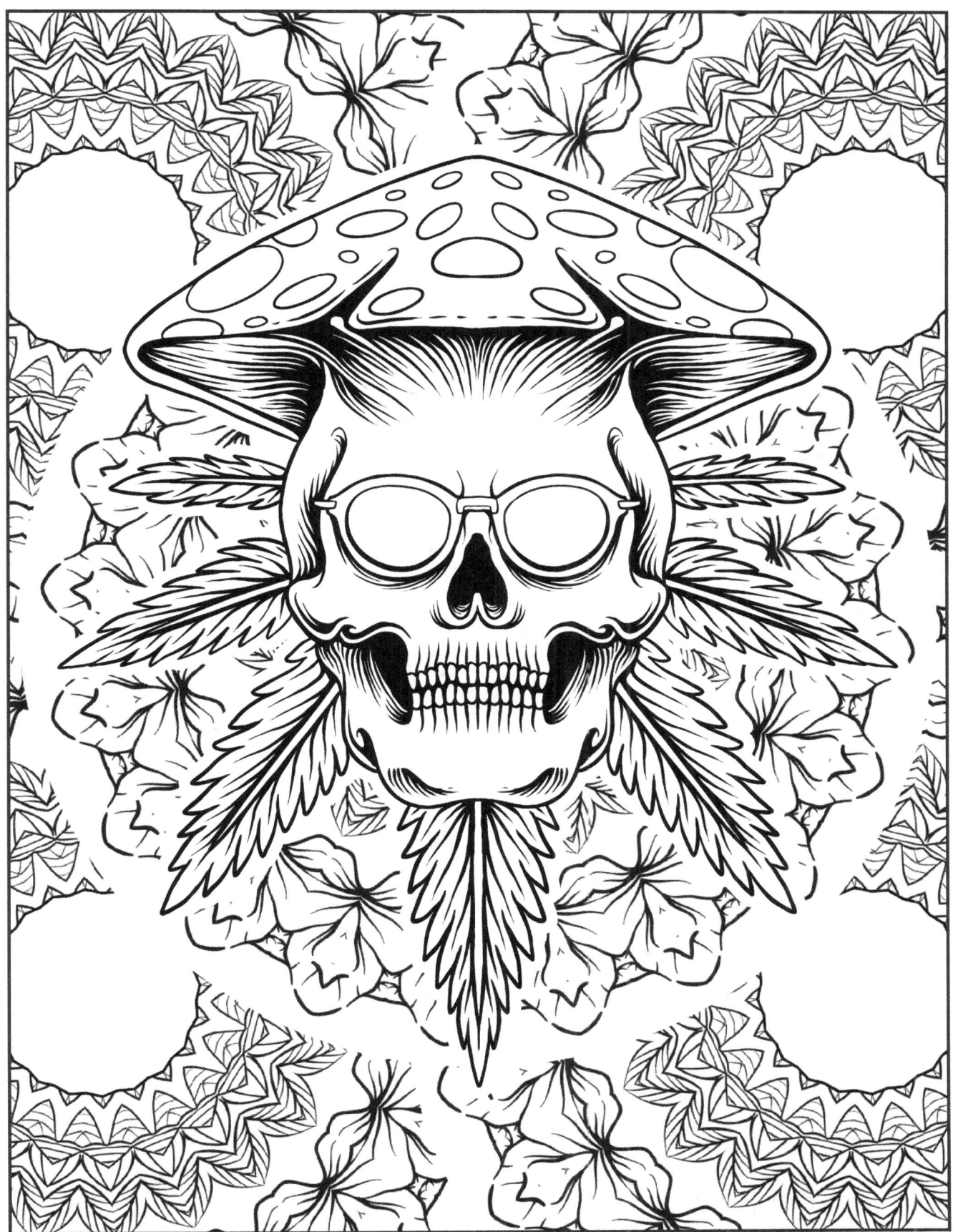

Copyright
R.U. Tokin and C.V. Designs

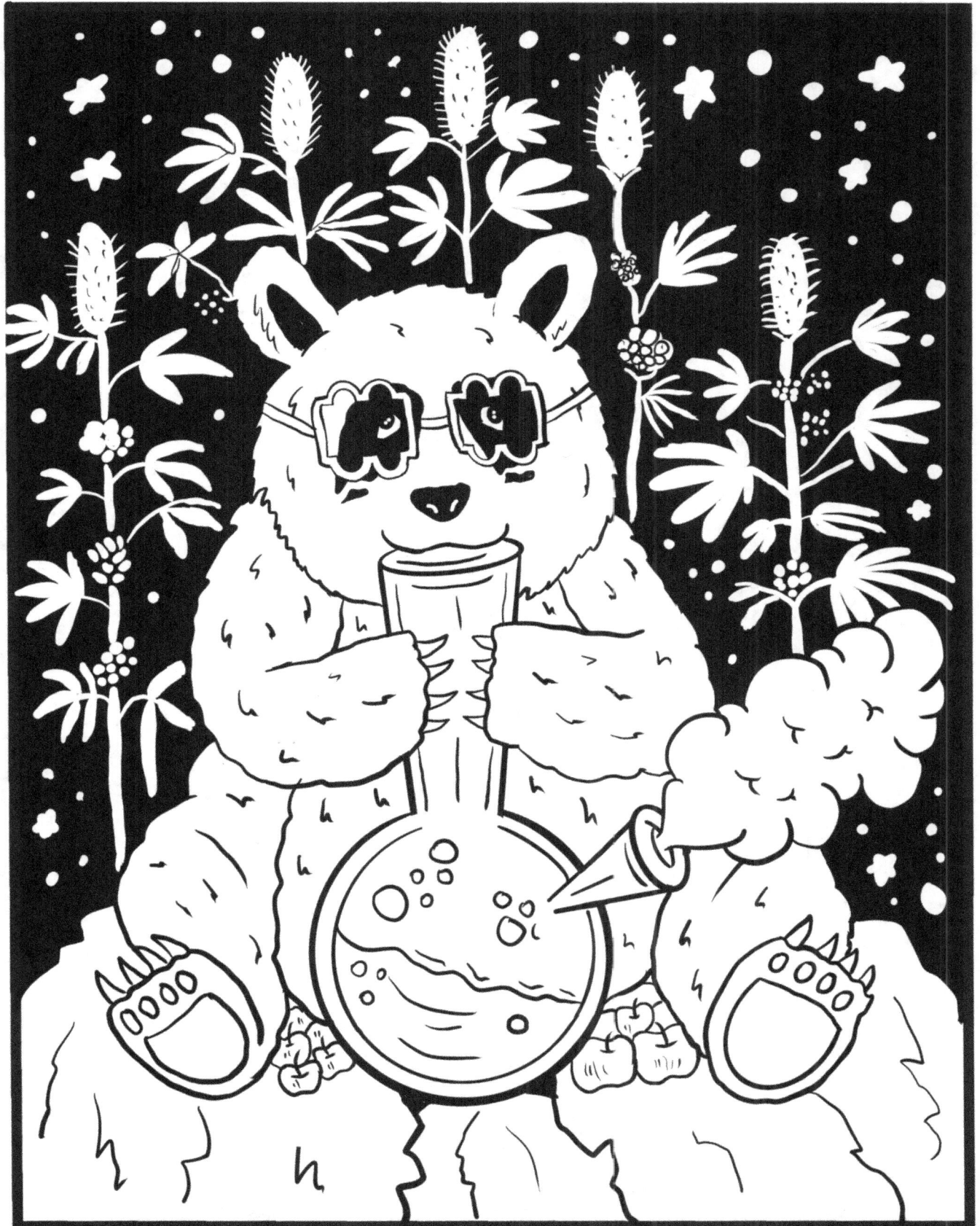

Copyright

R.U. Tokin and C.V. Designs

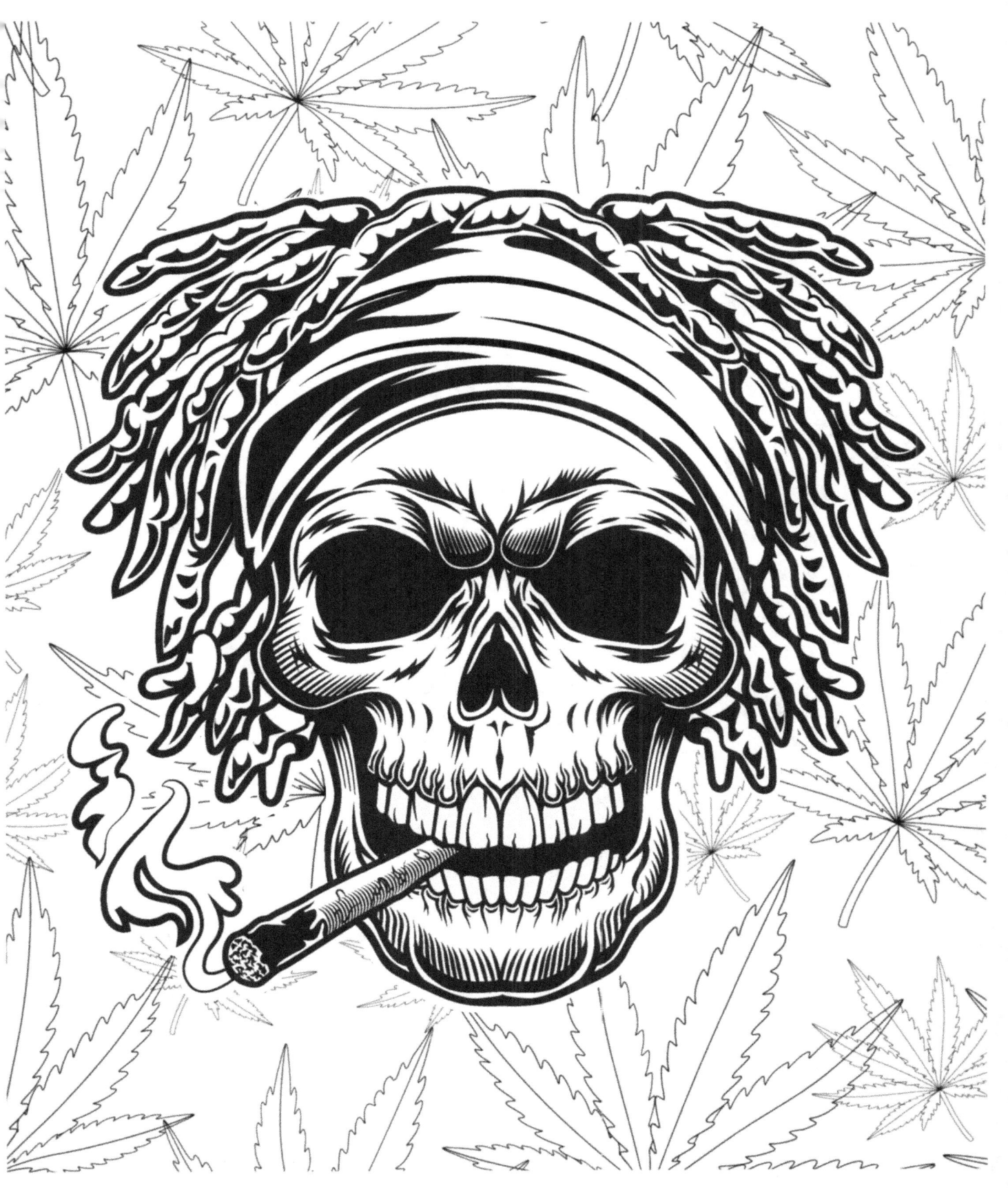

Copyright
R.U. Tokin and C.V. Designs

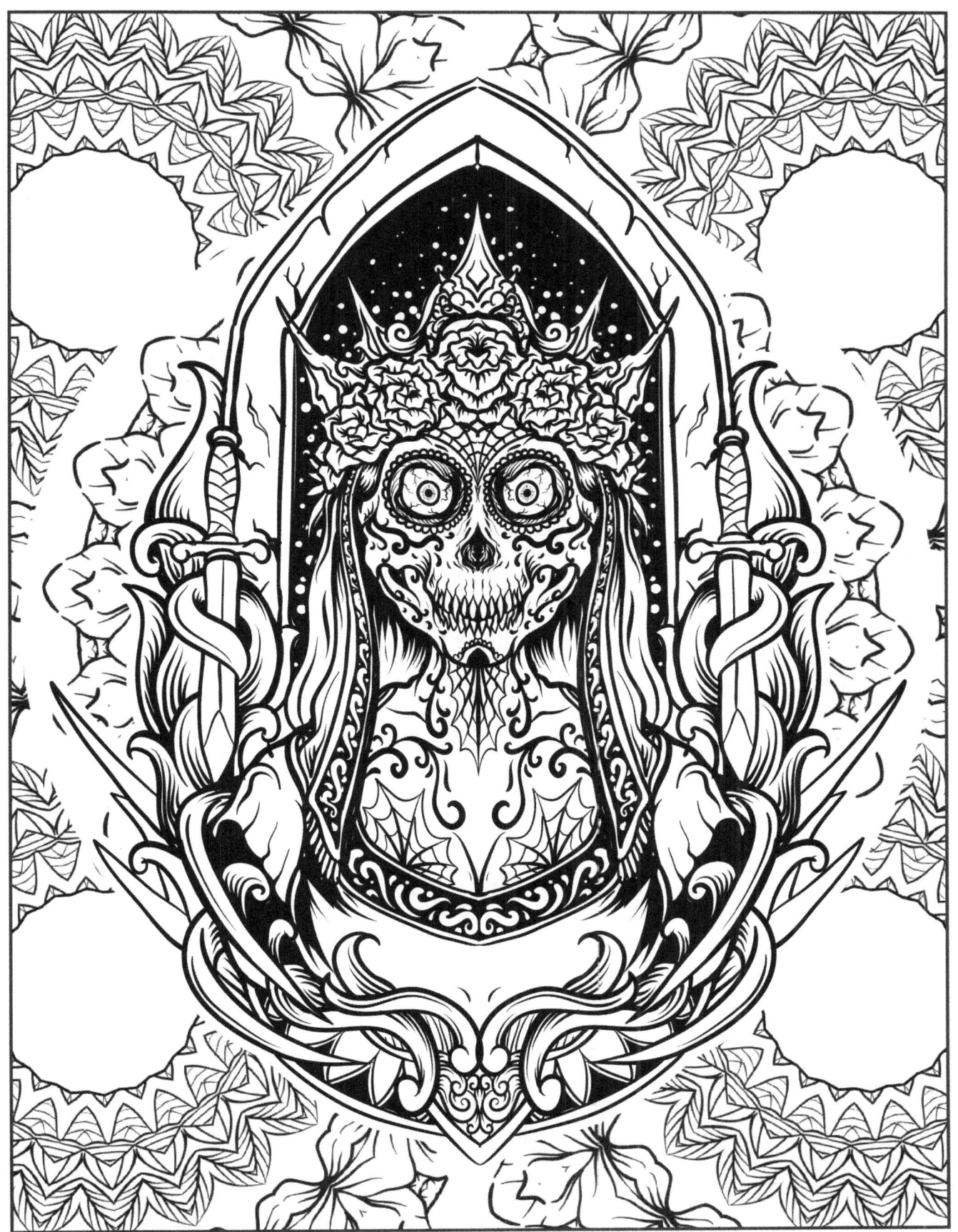

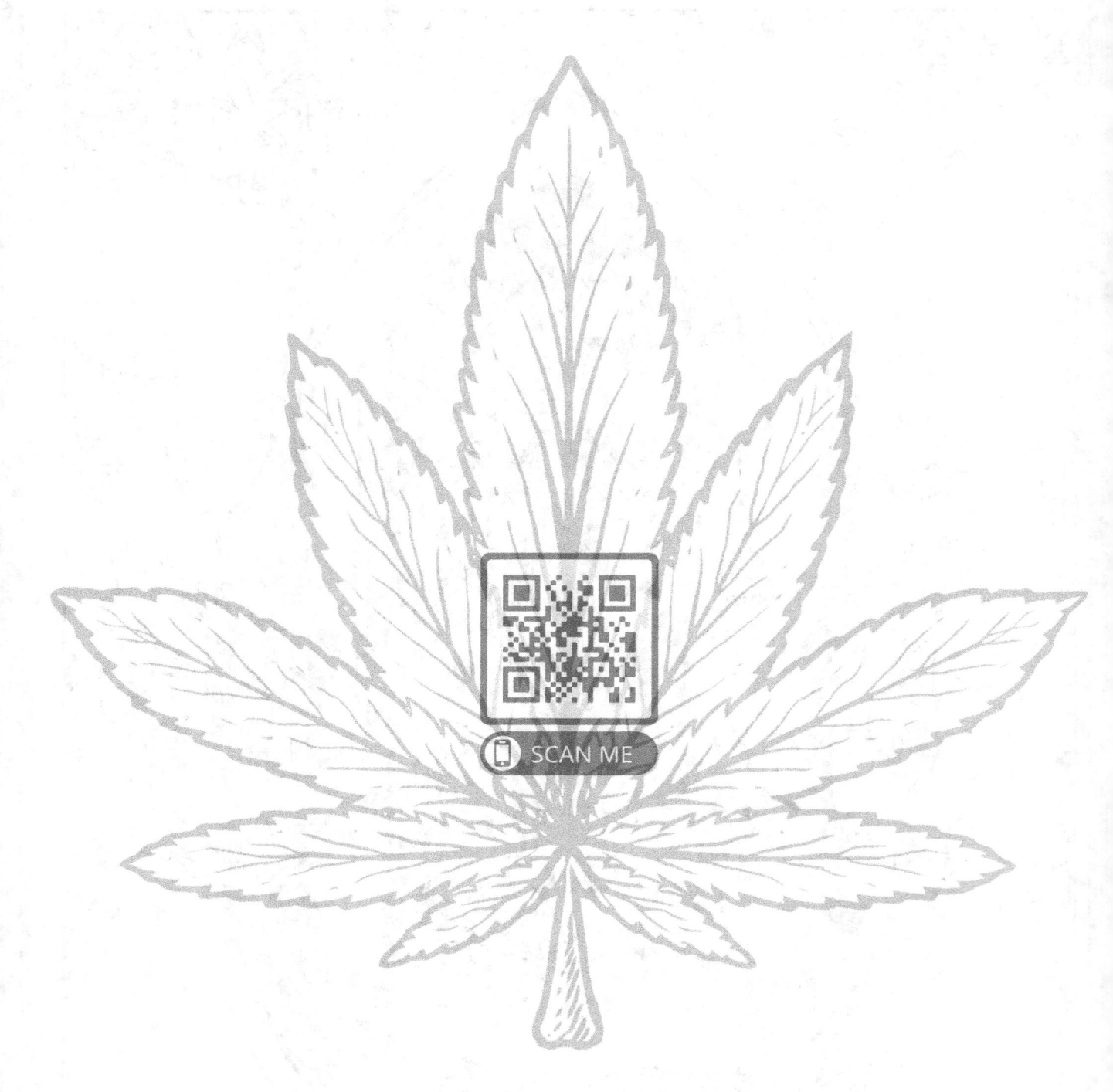

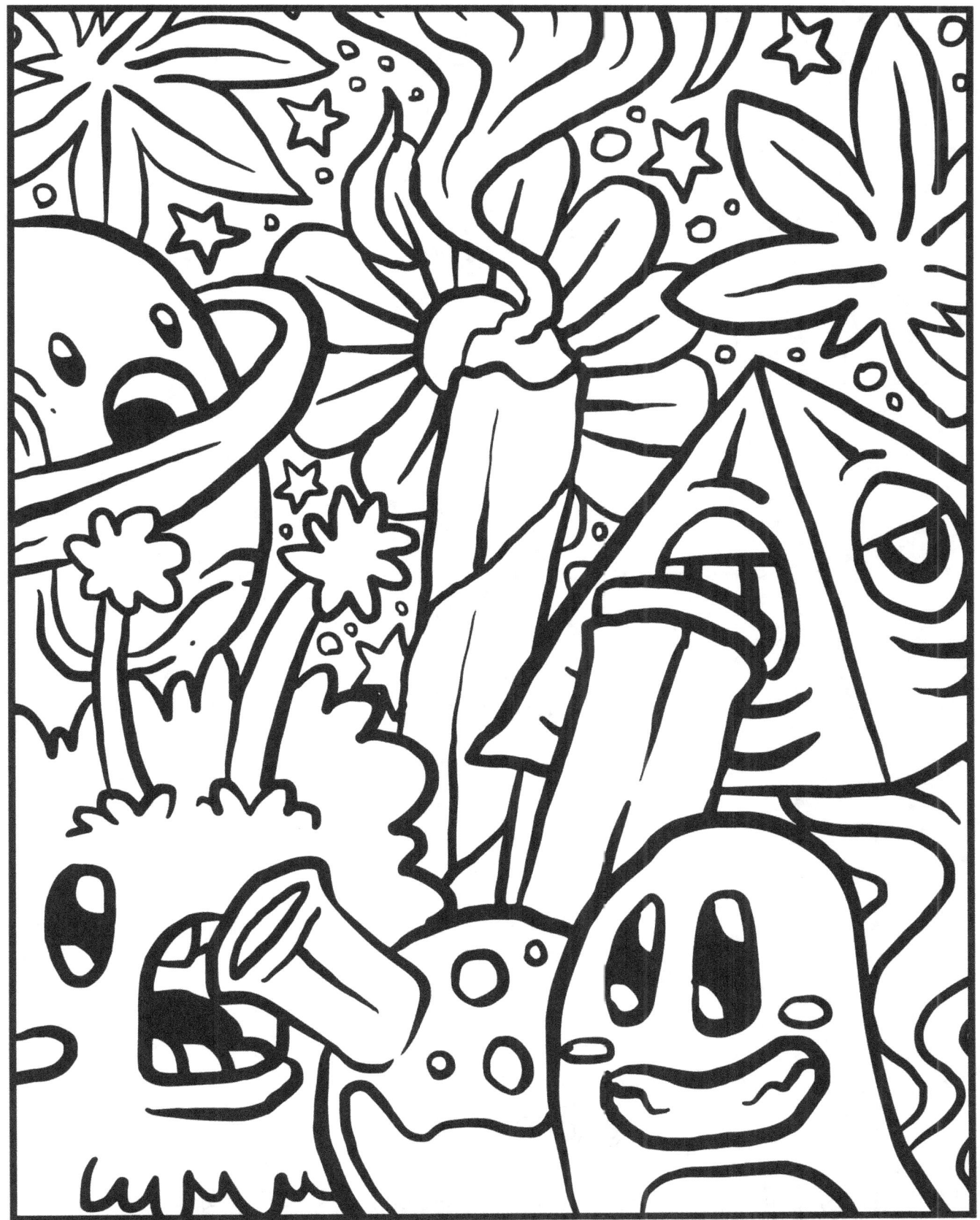

Copyright

R.U. Tokin and C.V. Designs

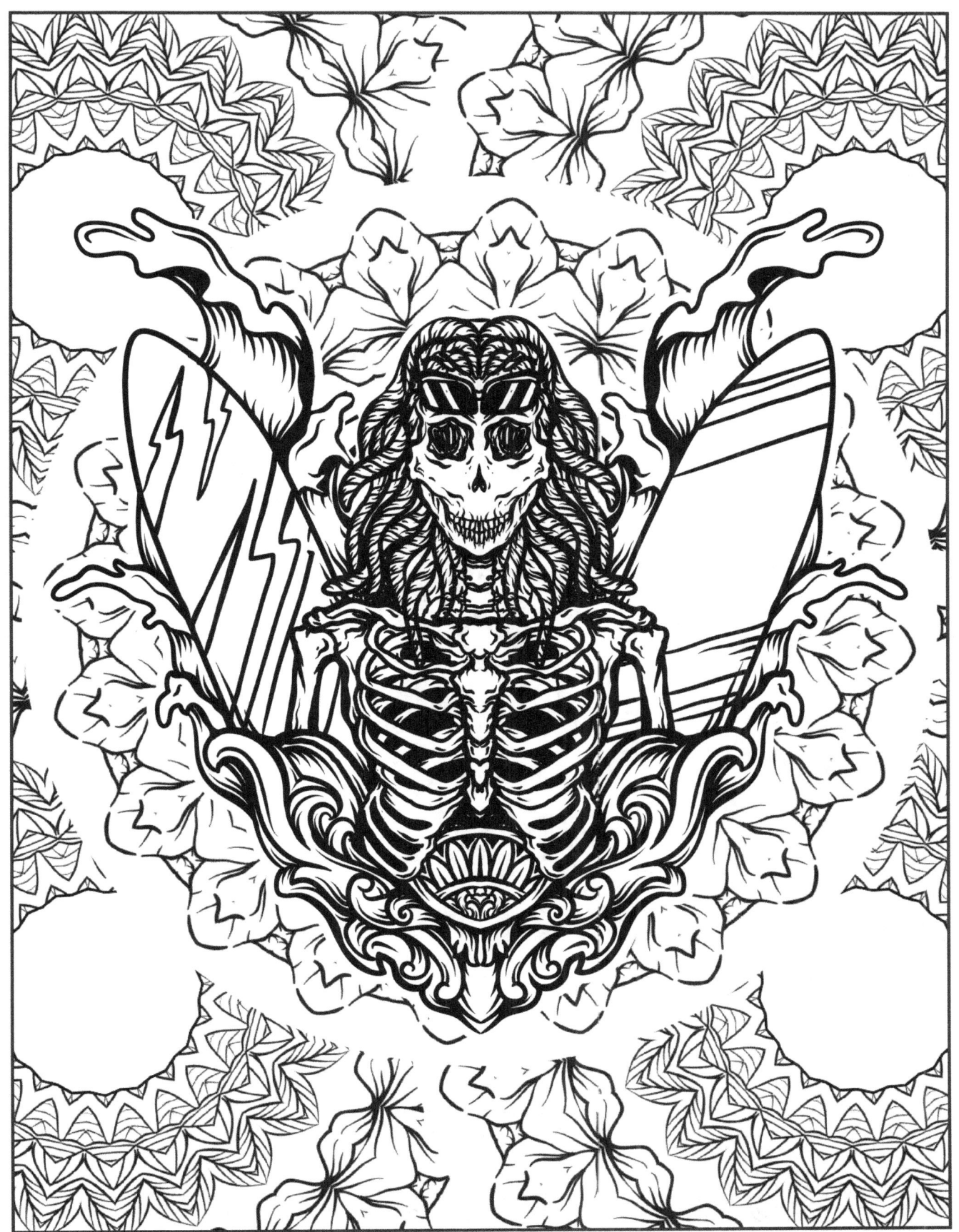

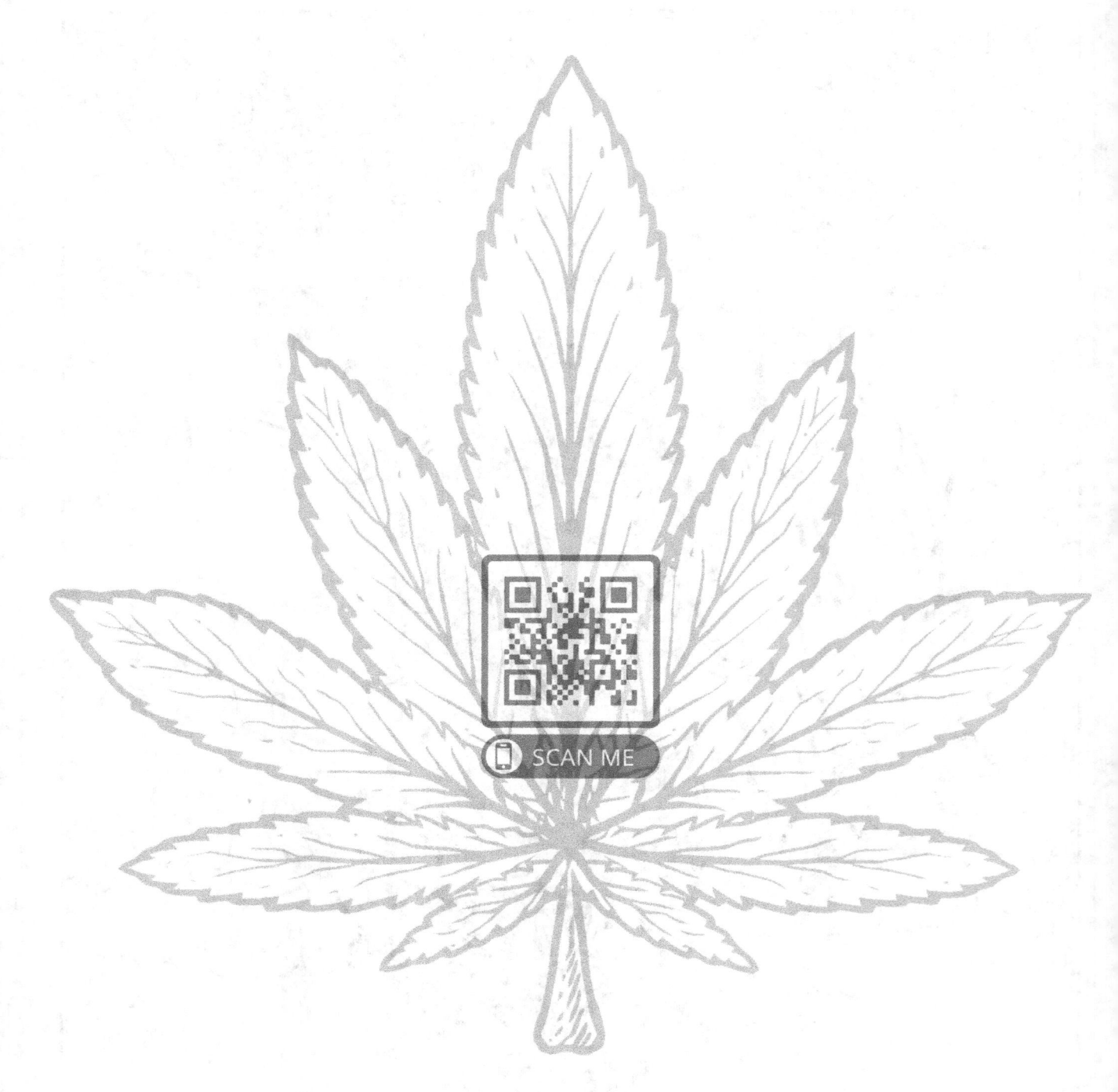

Copyright

R.U. Tokin and C.V. Designs

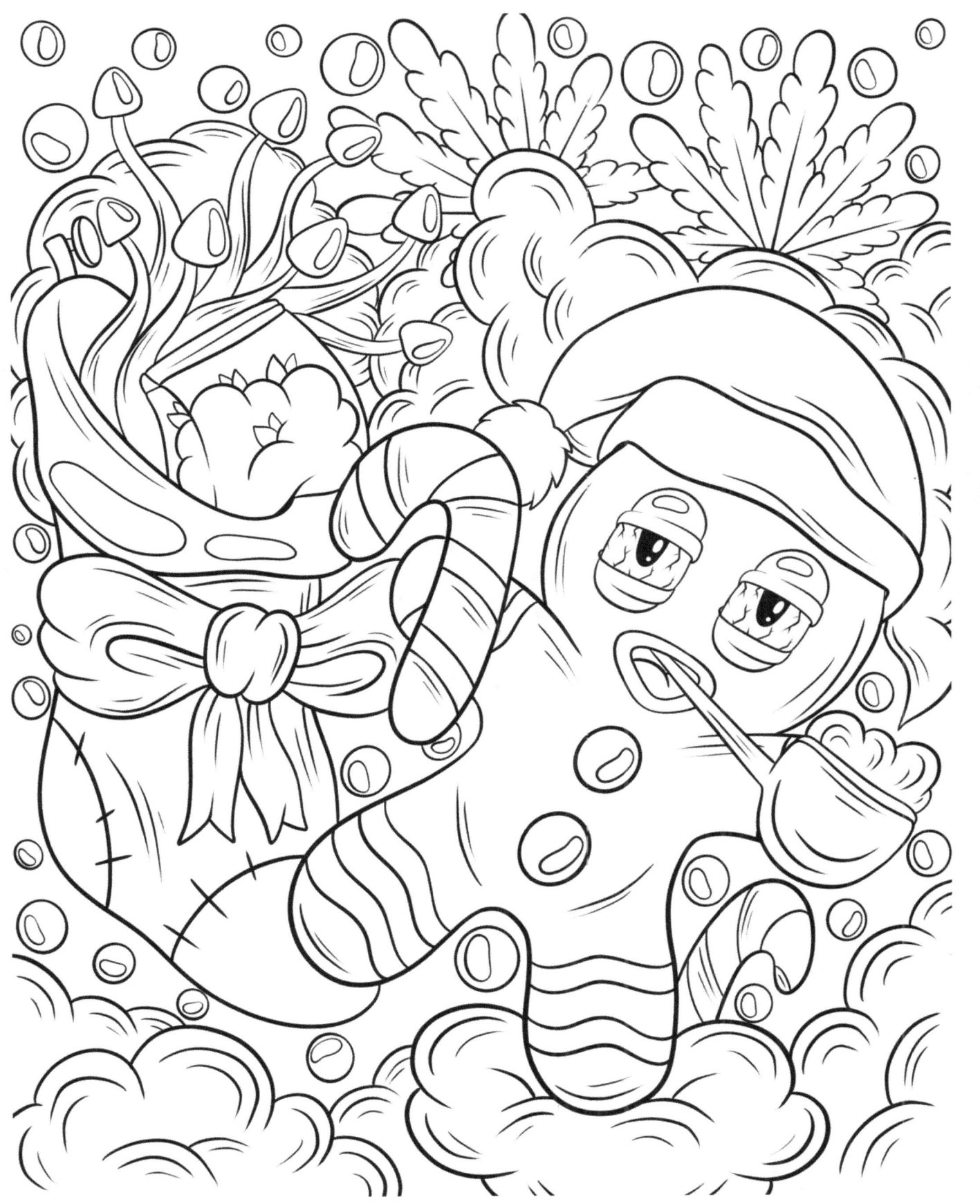

Copyright
R.U. Tokin and C.V. Designs

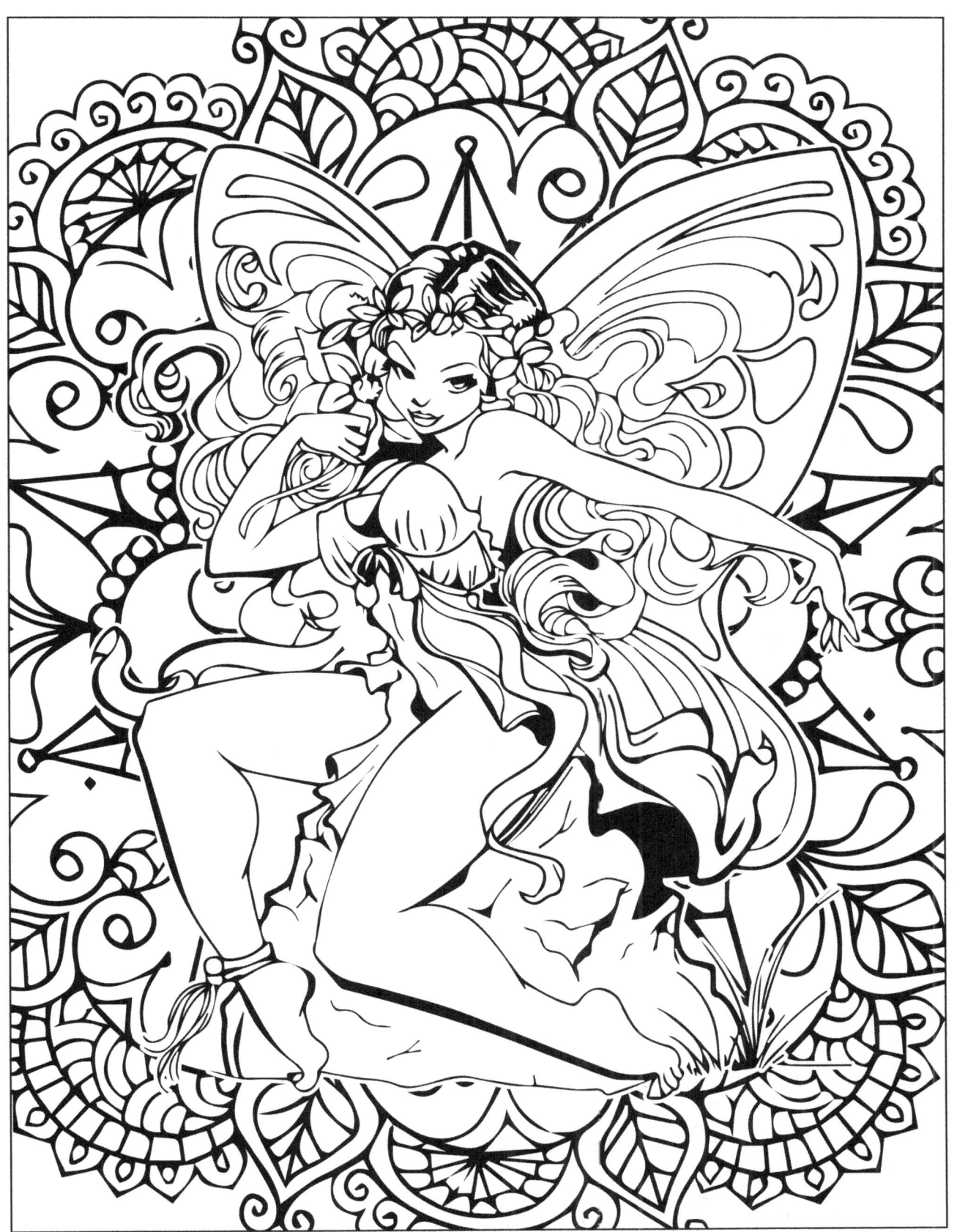

Copyright

R.U. Tokin and C.V. Designs

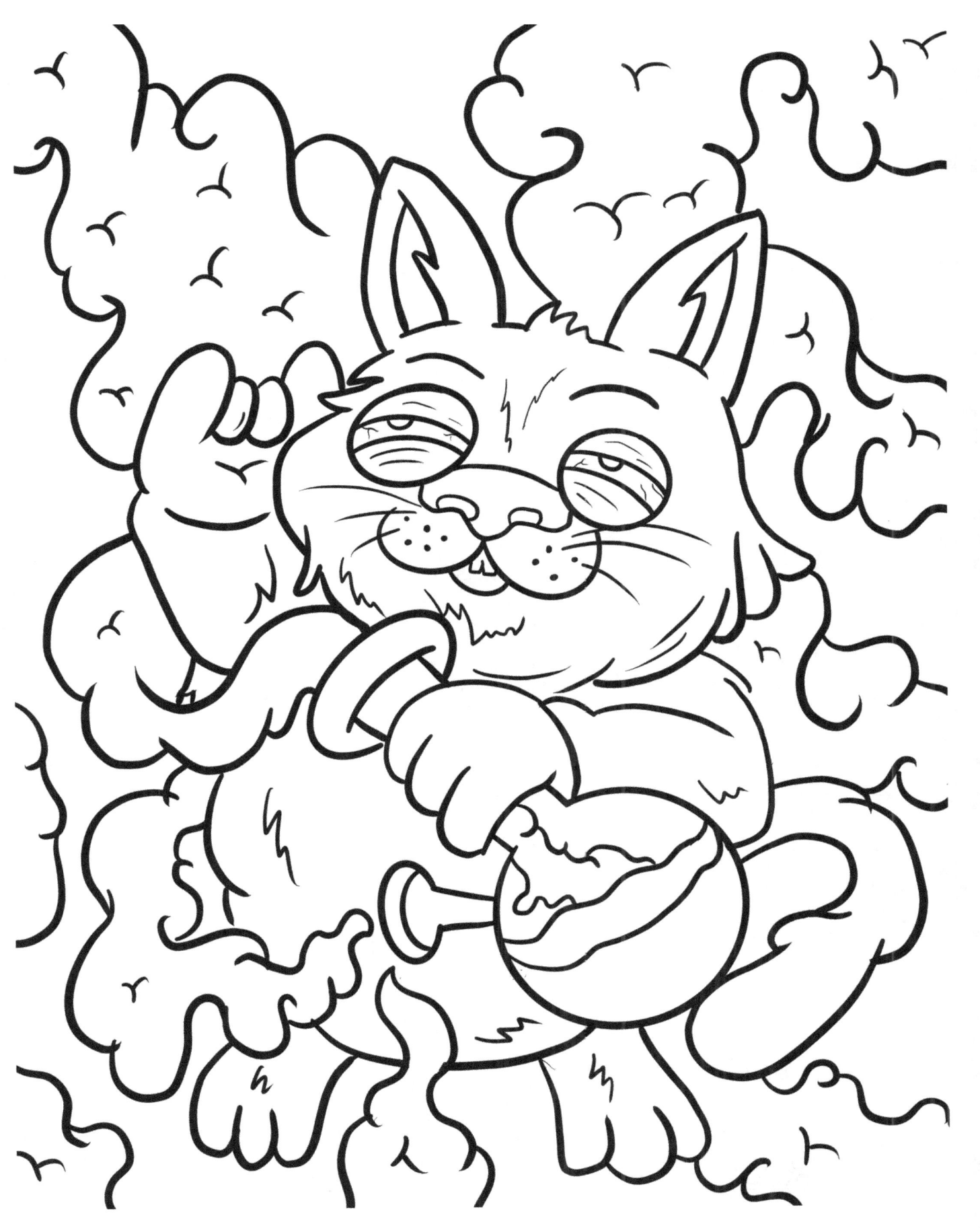

Copyright

R.U. Tokin and C.V. Designs

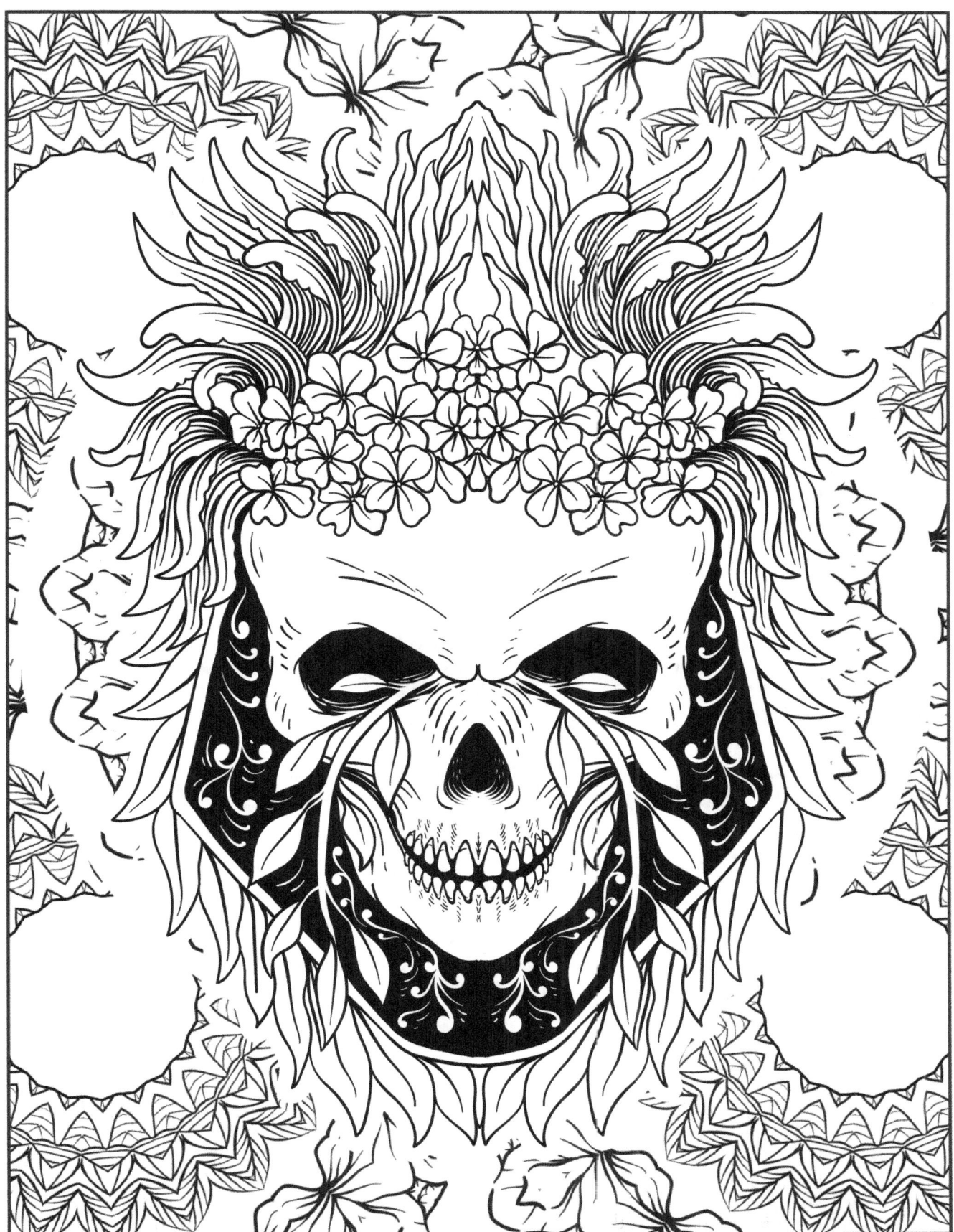

Copyright

R.U. Tokin and C.V. Designs

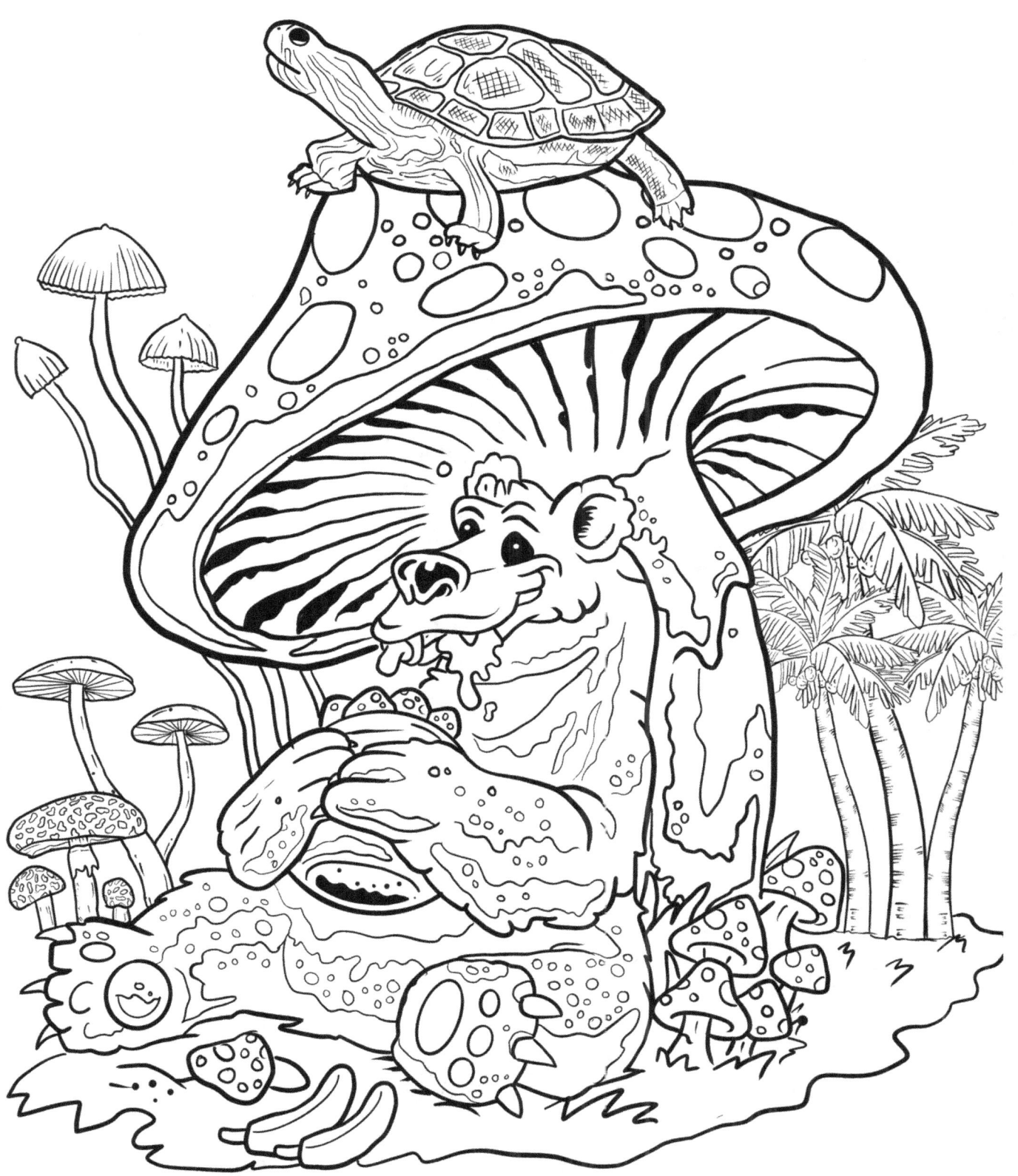

Copyright
R.U. Tokin and C.V. Designs

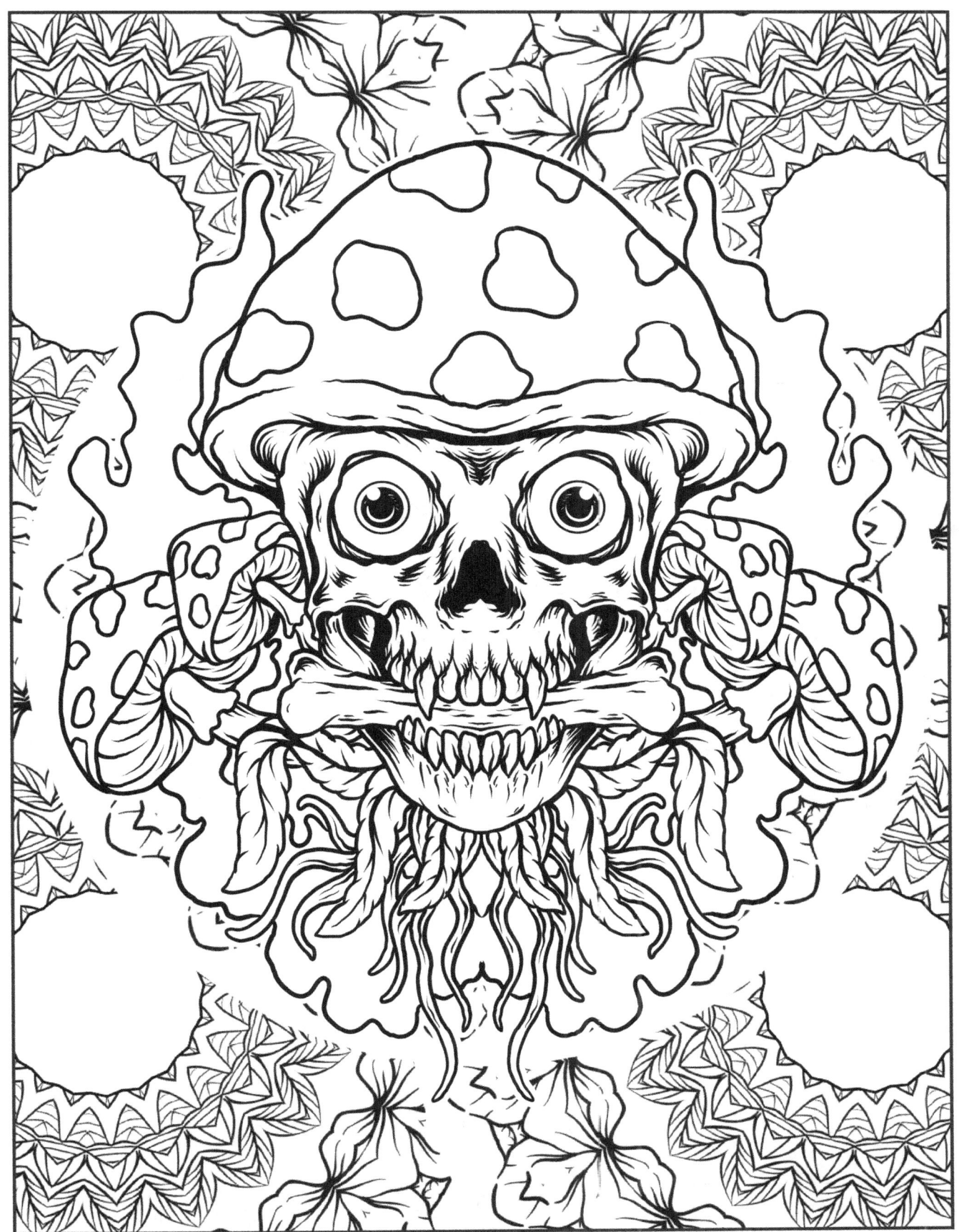

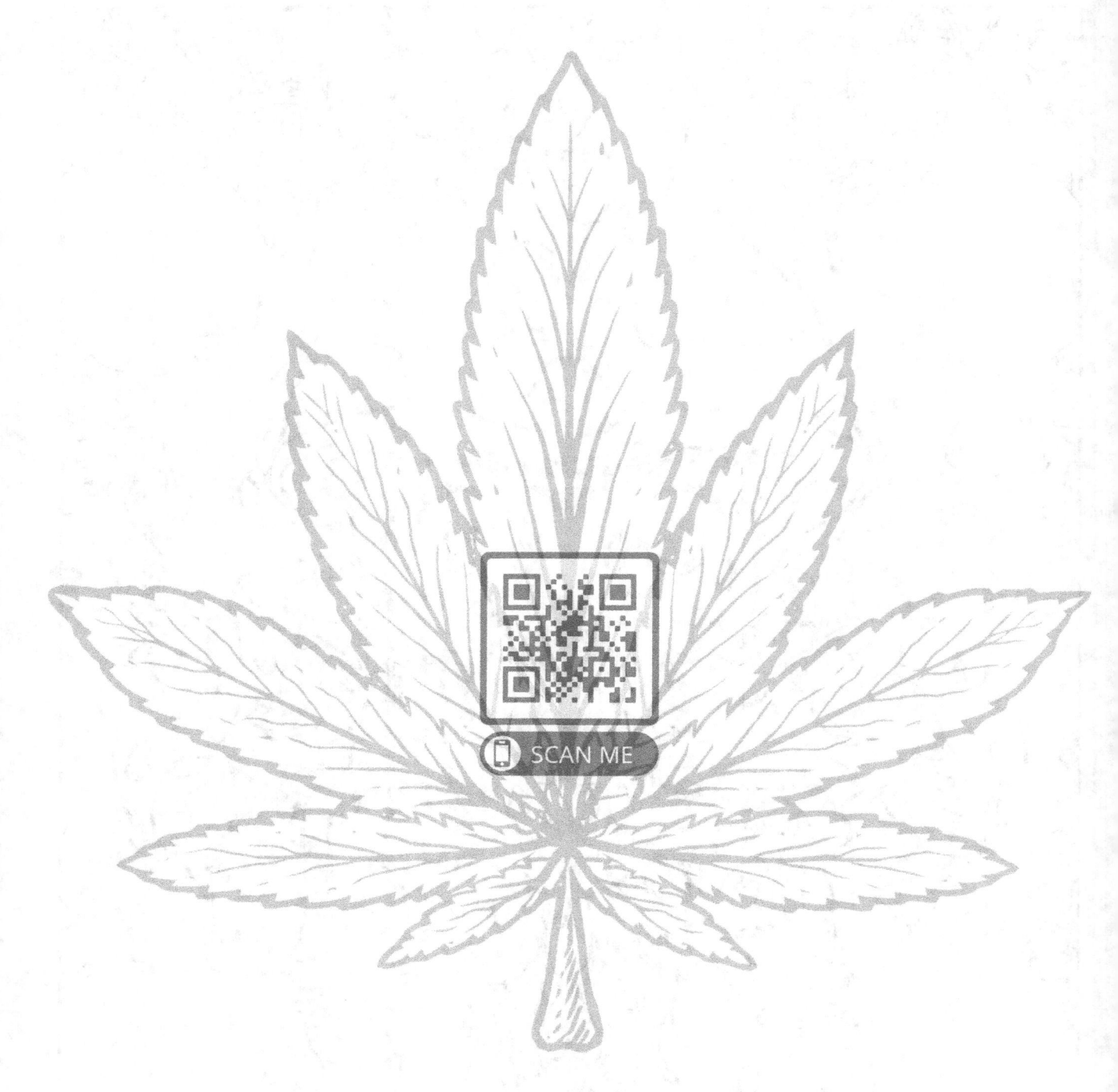

Copyright

R.U. Tokin and C.V. Designs

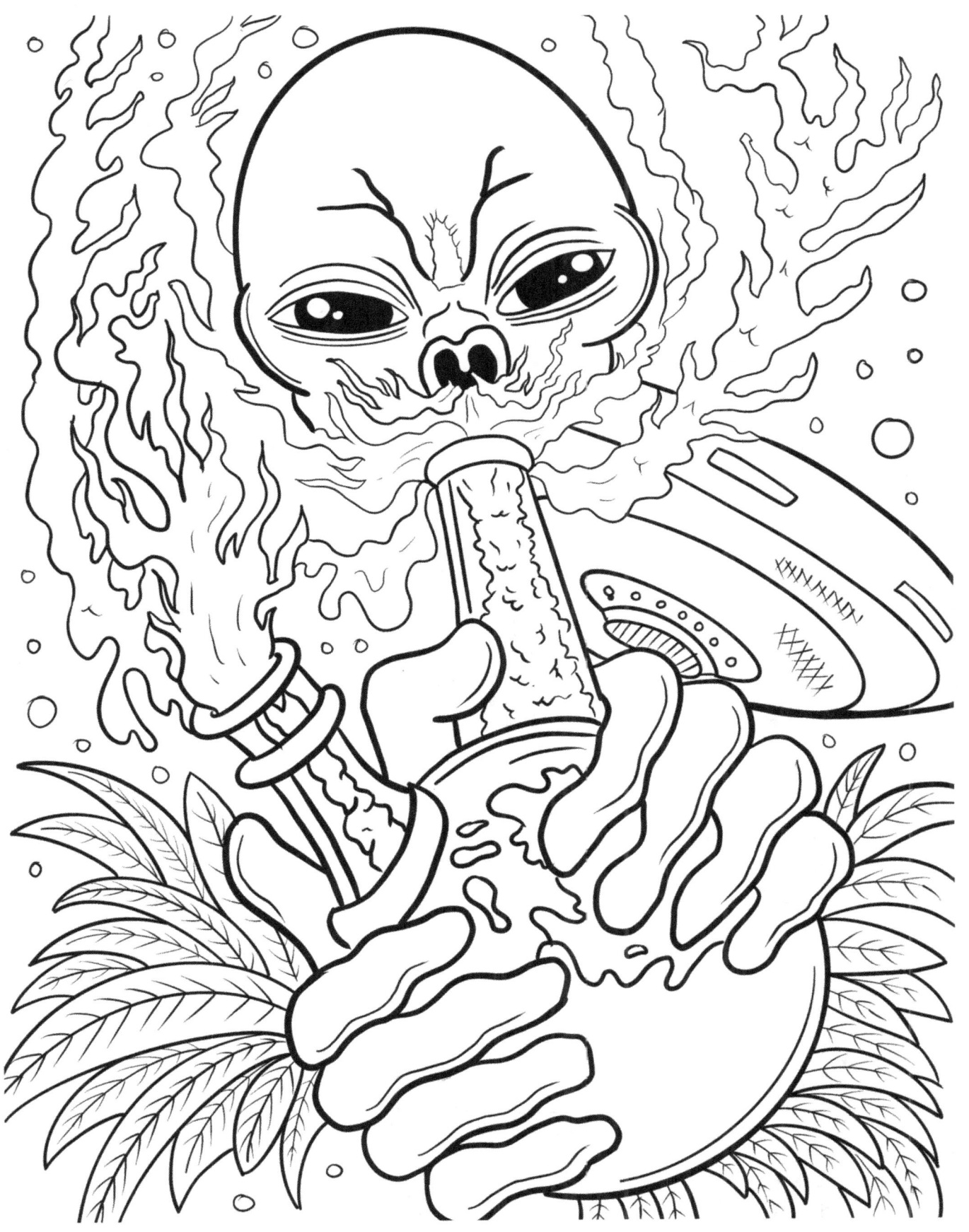

Copyright
R.U. Tokin and C.V. Designs

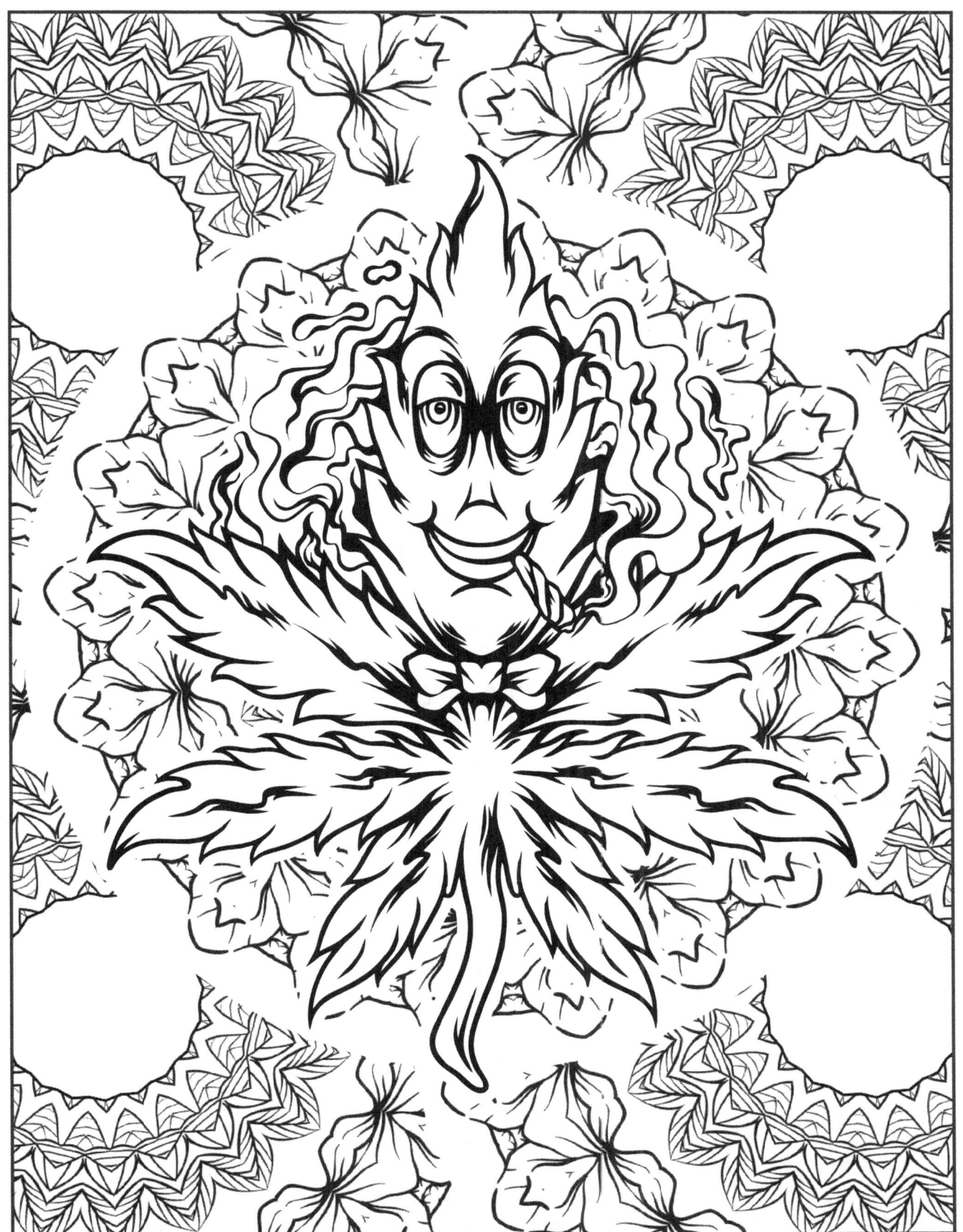

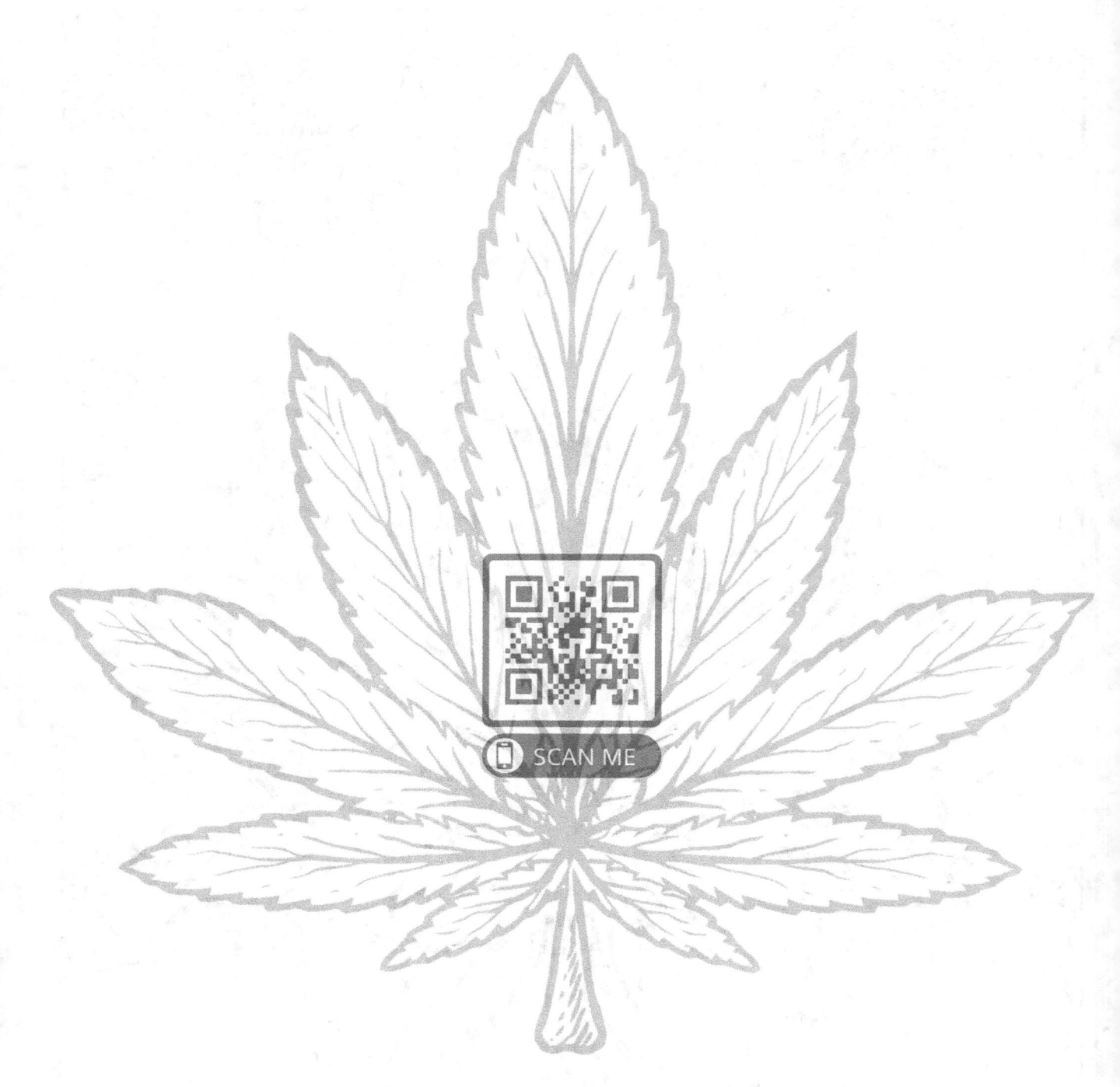

Copyright

R.U. Tokin and C.V. Designs

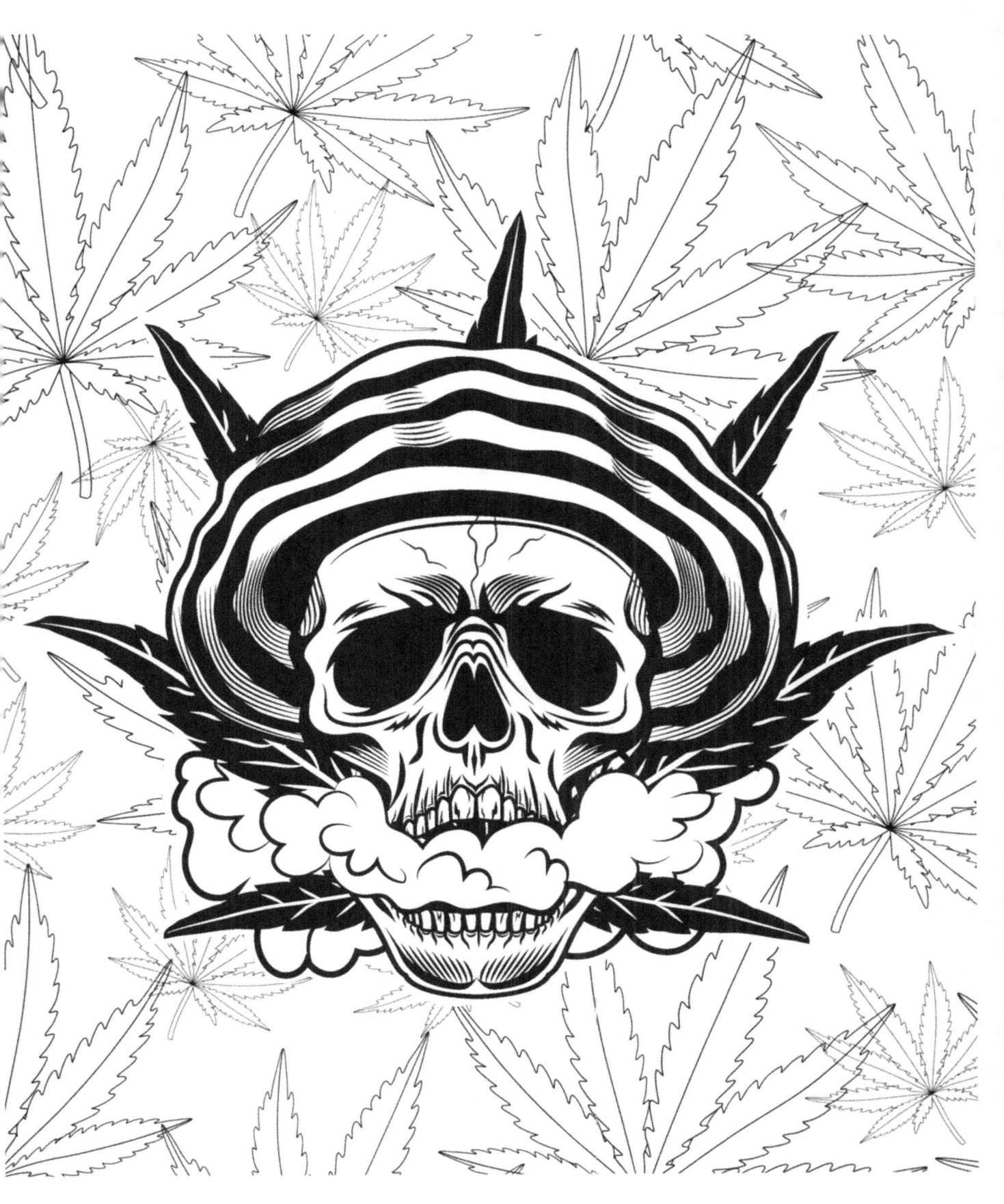

Copyright
R.U. Tokin and C.V. Designs

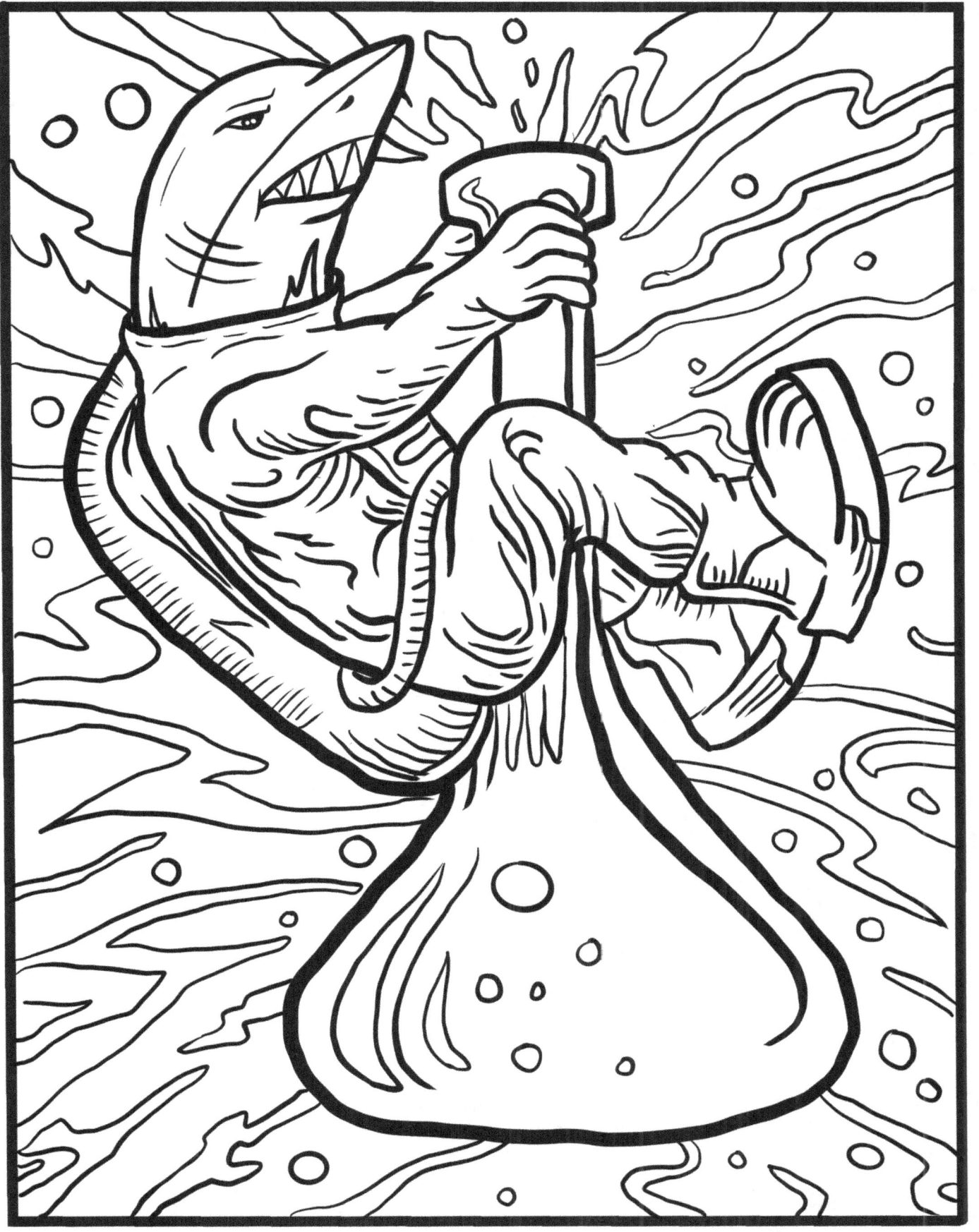

Copyright
R.U. Tokin and C.V. Designs

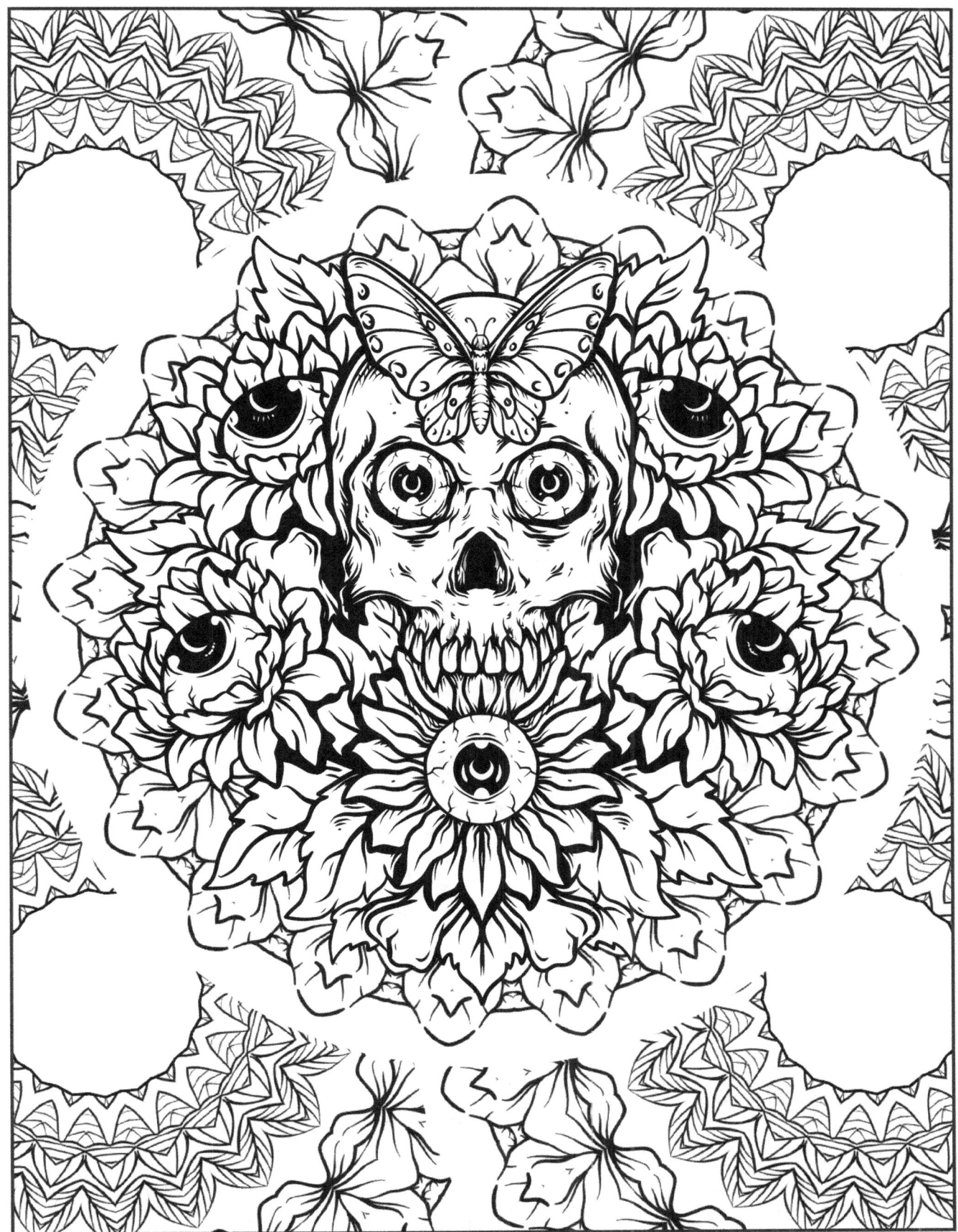

Copyright

R.U. Tokin and C.V. Designs

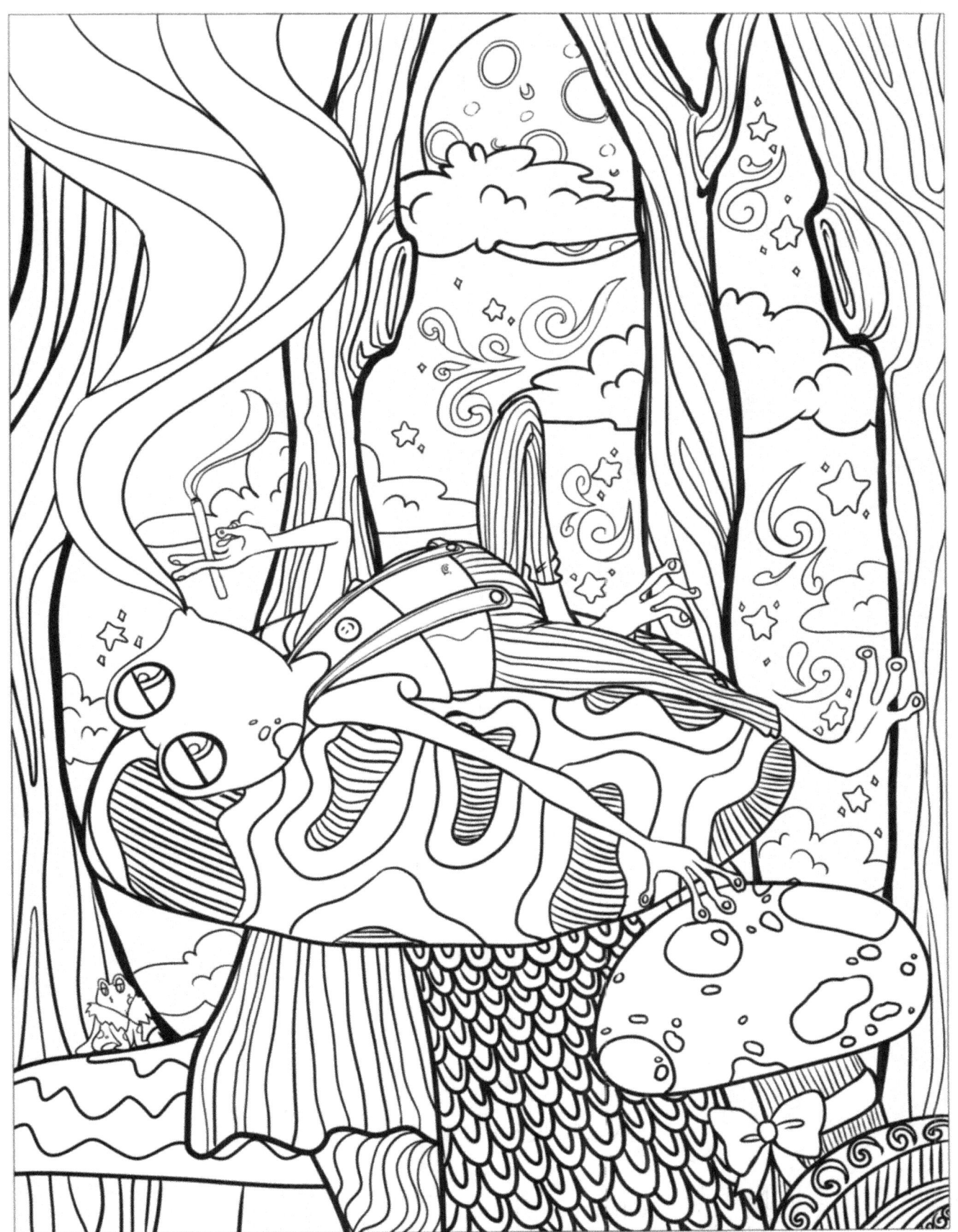

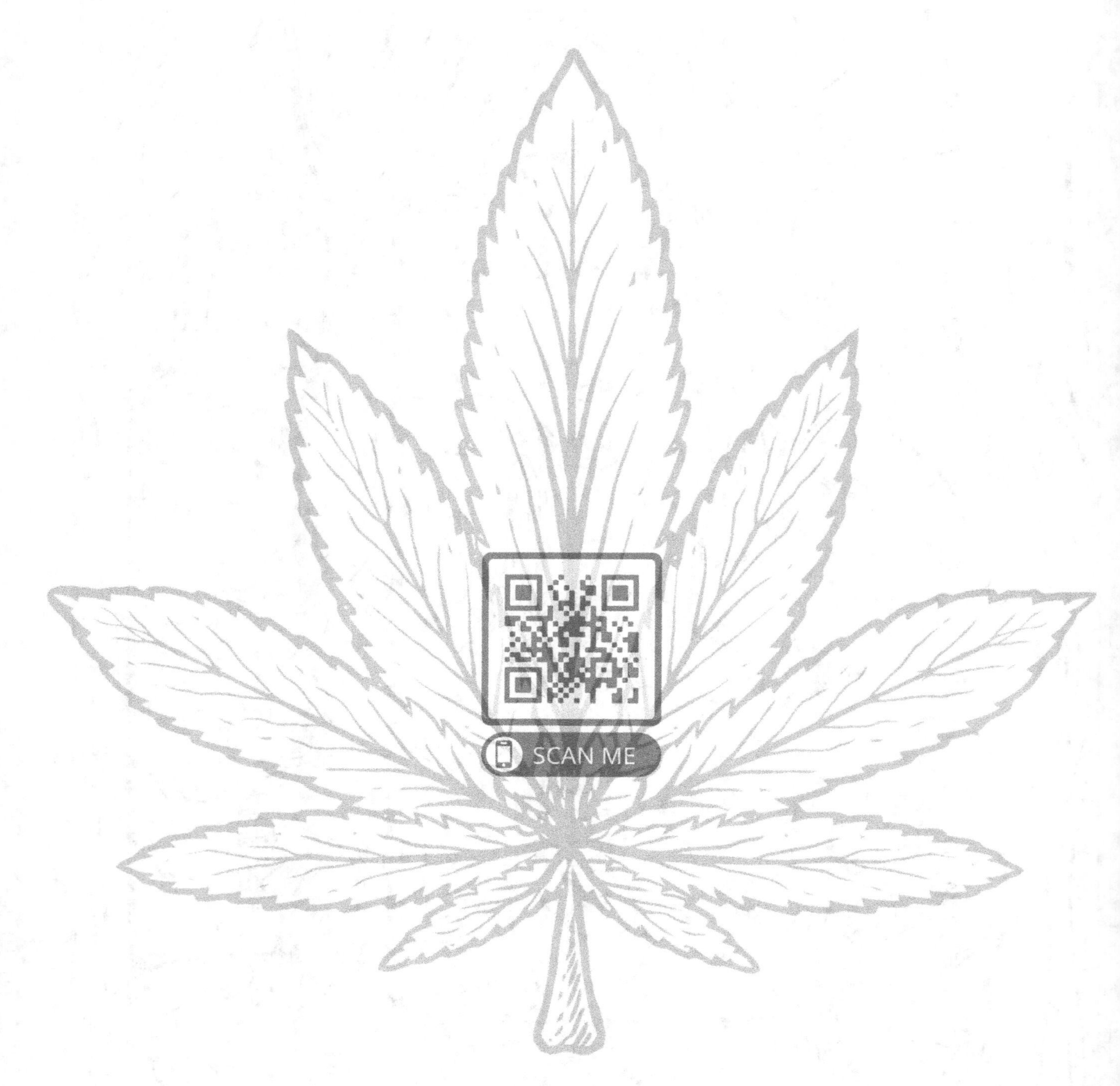

Copyright
R.U. Tokin and C.V. Designs

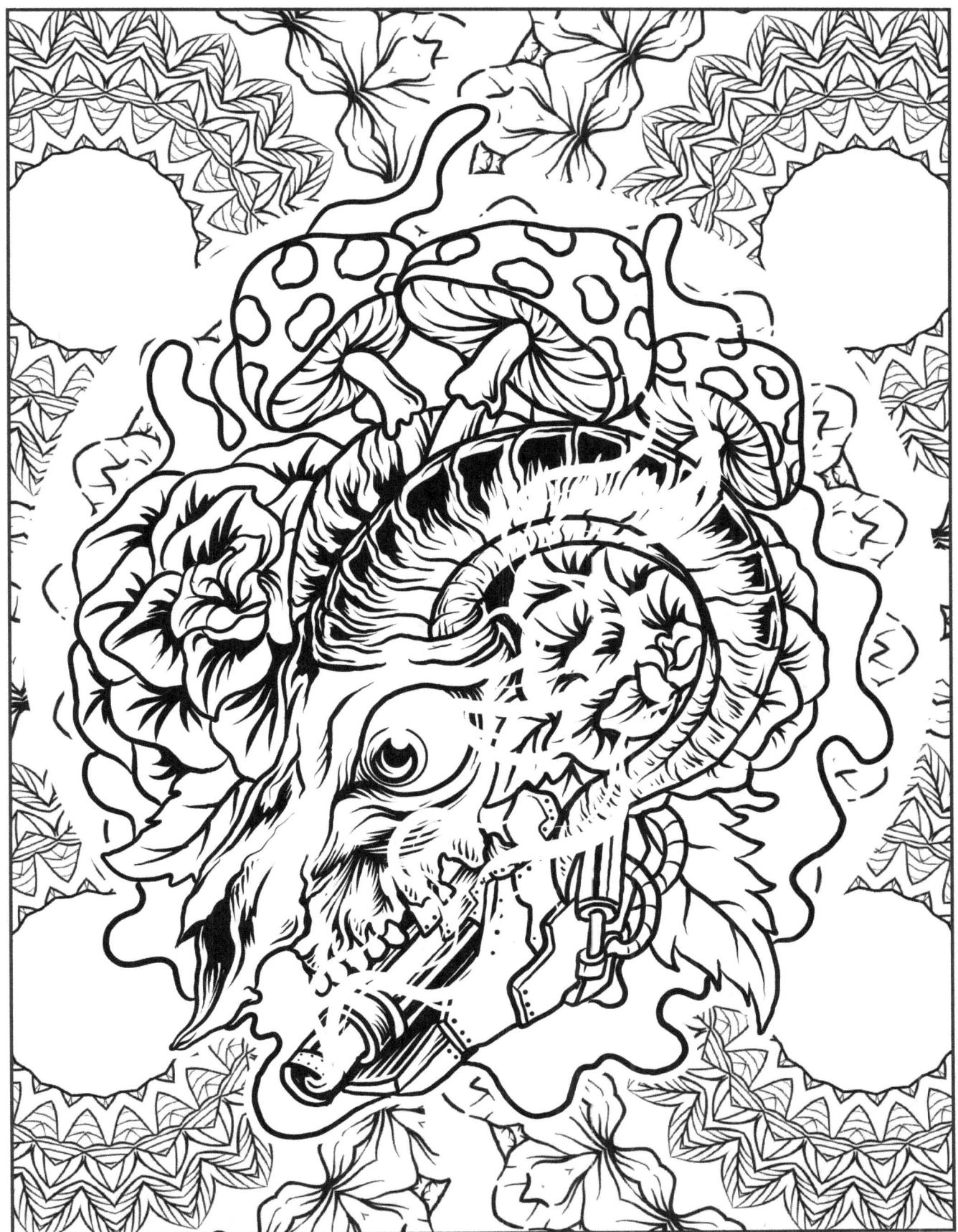

Copyright

R.U. Tokin and C.V. Designs

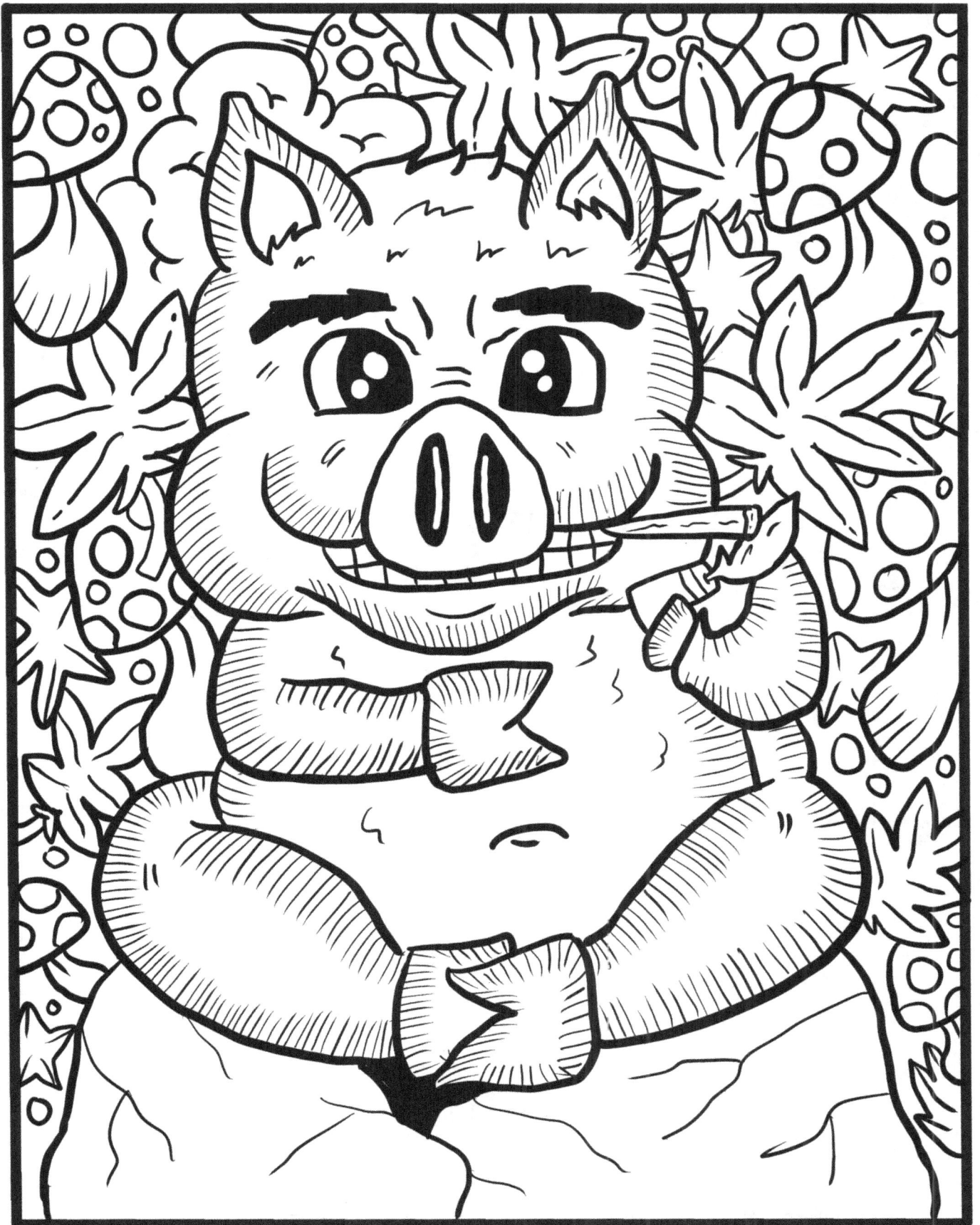

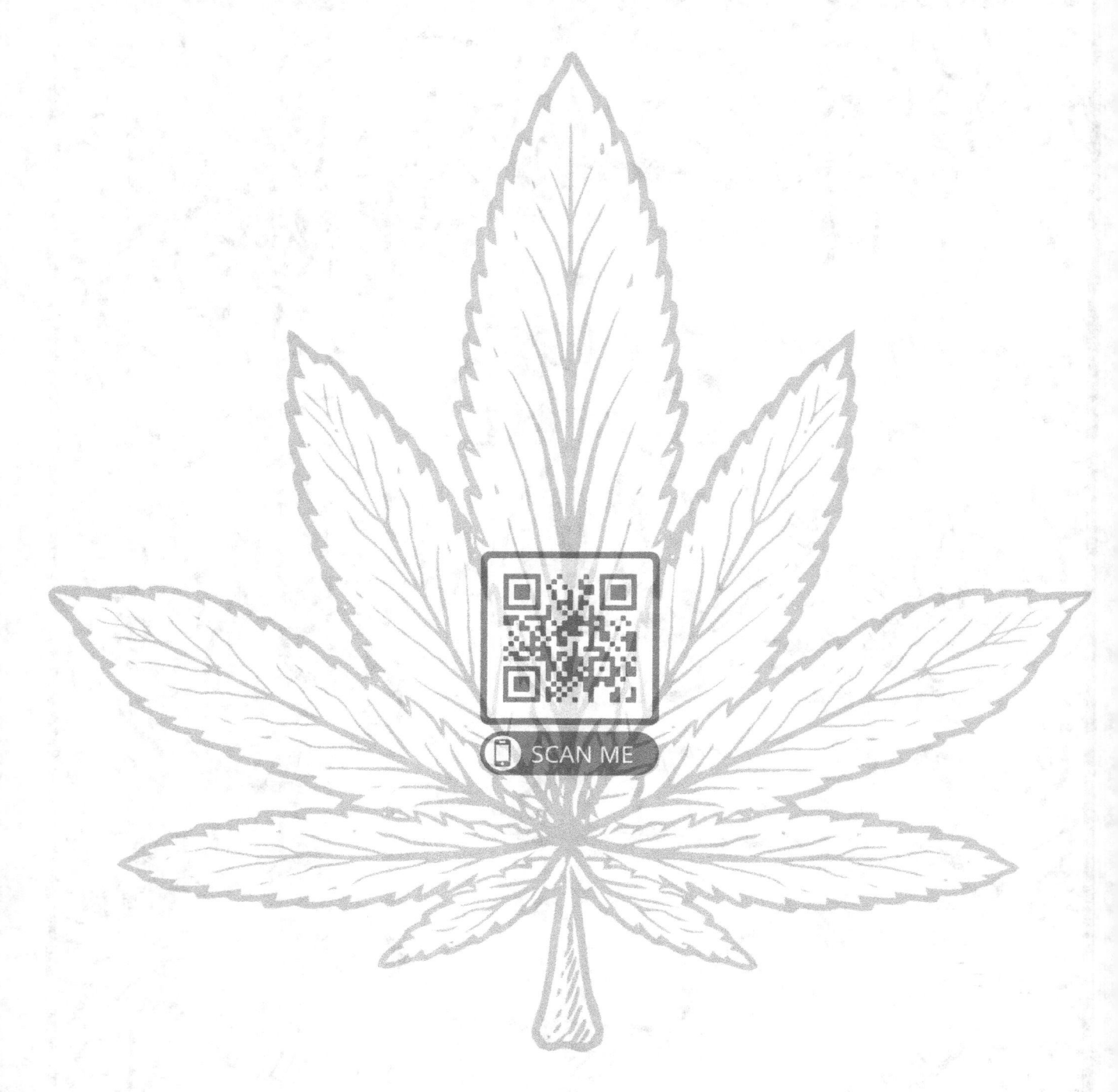

Copyright

R.U. Tokin and C.V. Designs

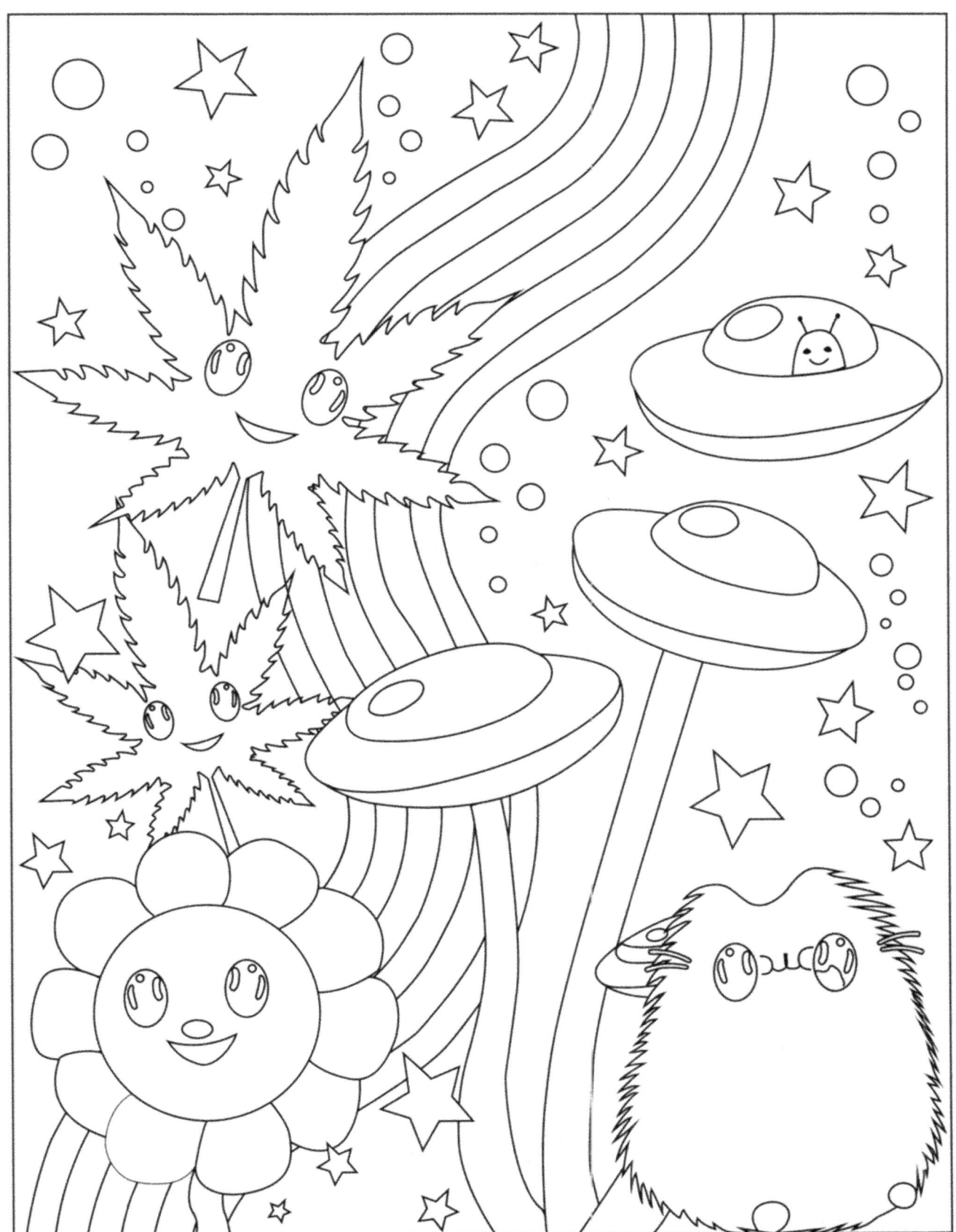

Copyright

R.U. Tokin and C.V. Designs

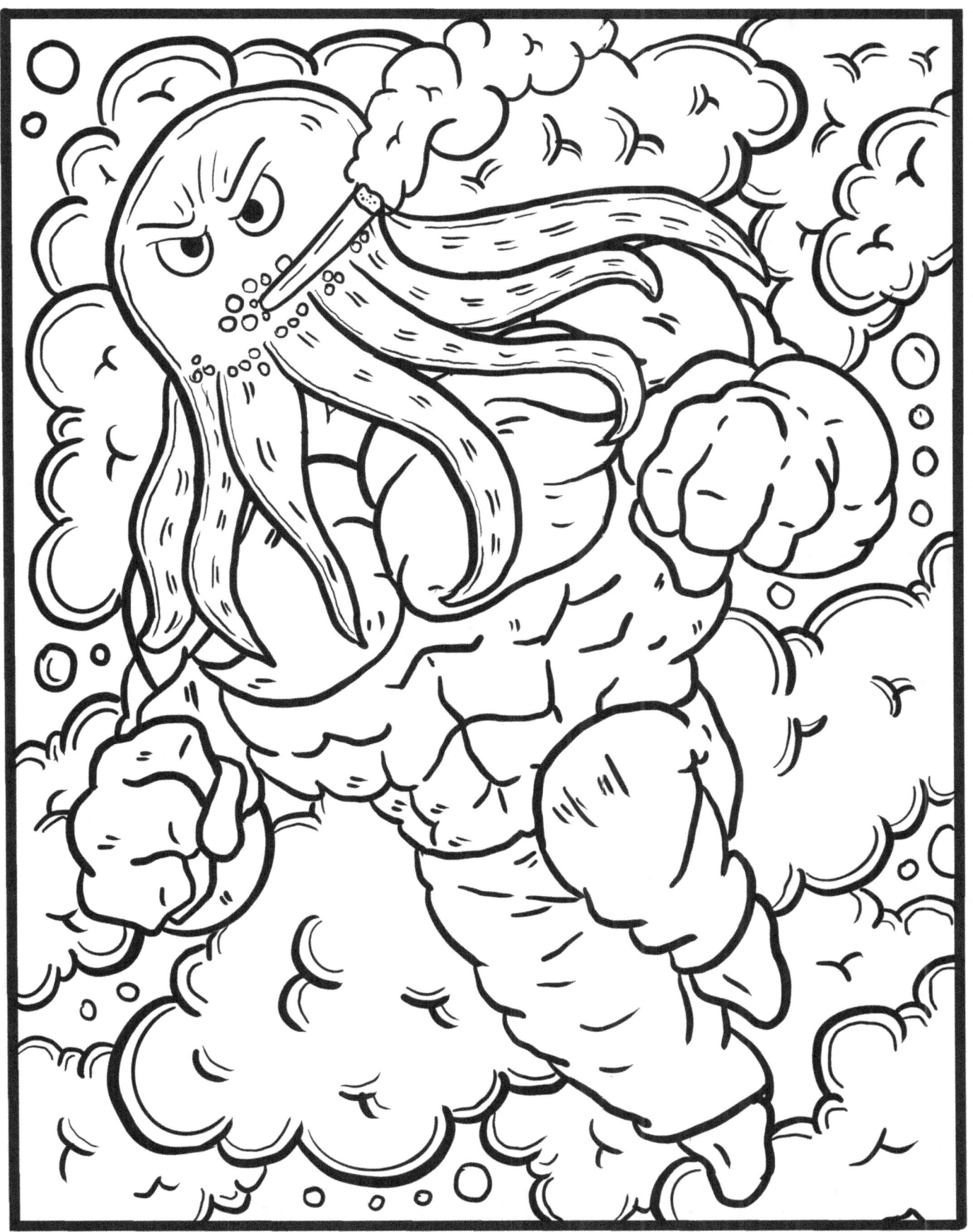

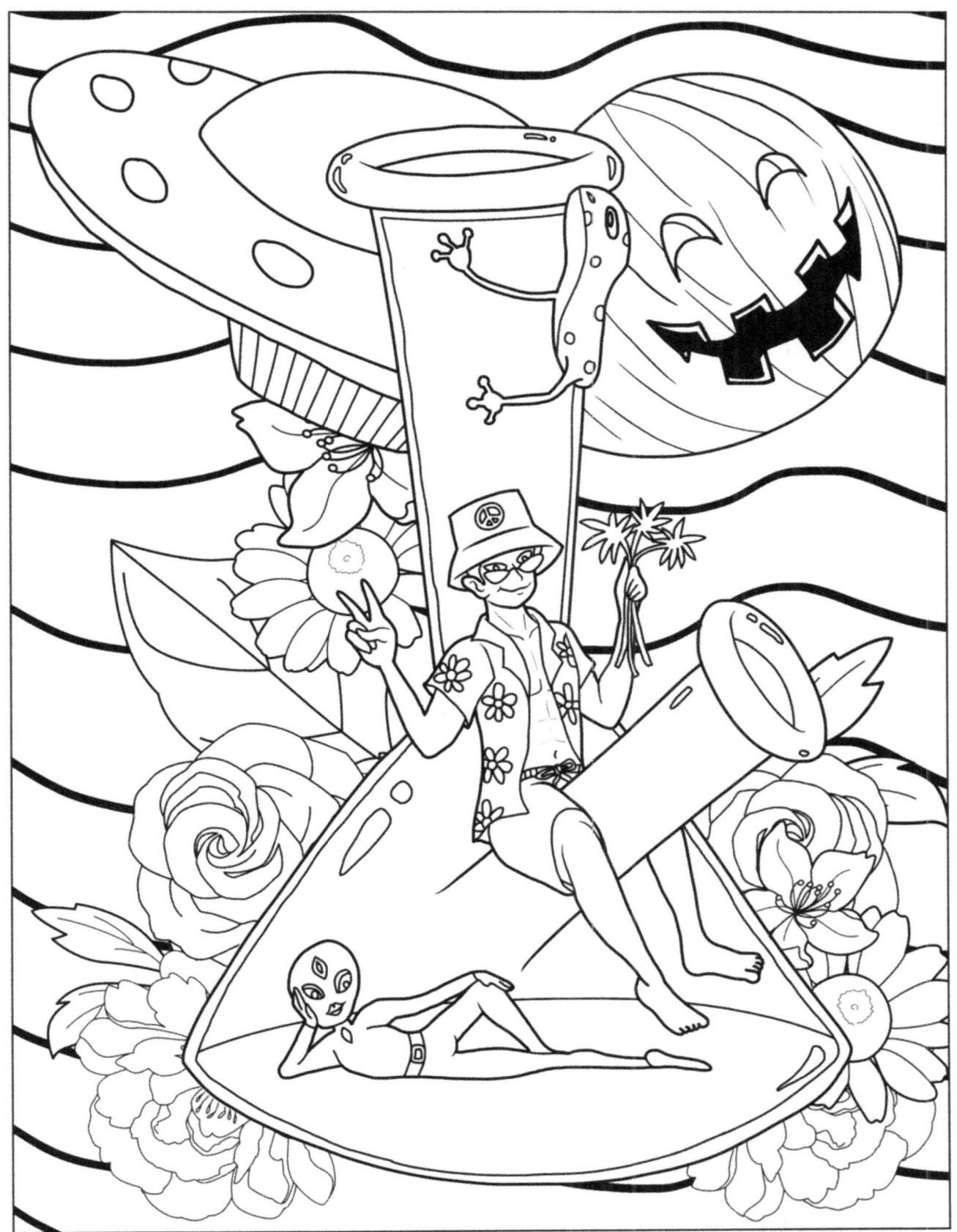

Copyright
R.U. Tokin and C.V. Designs

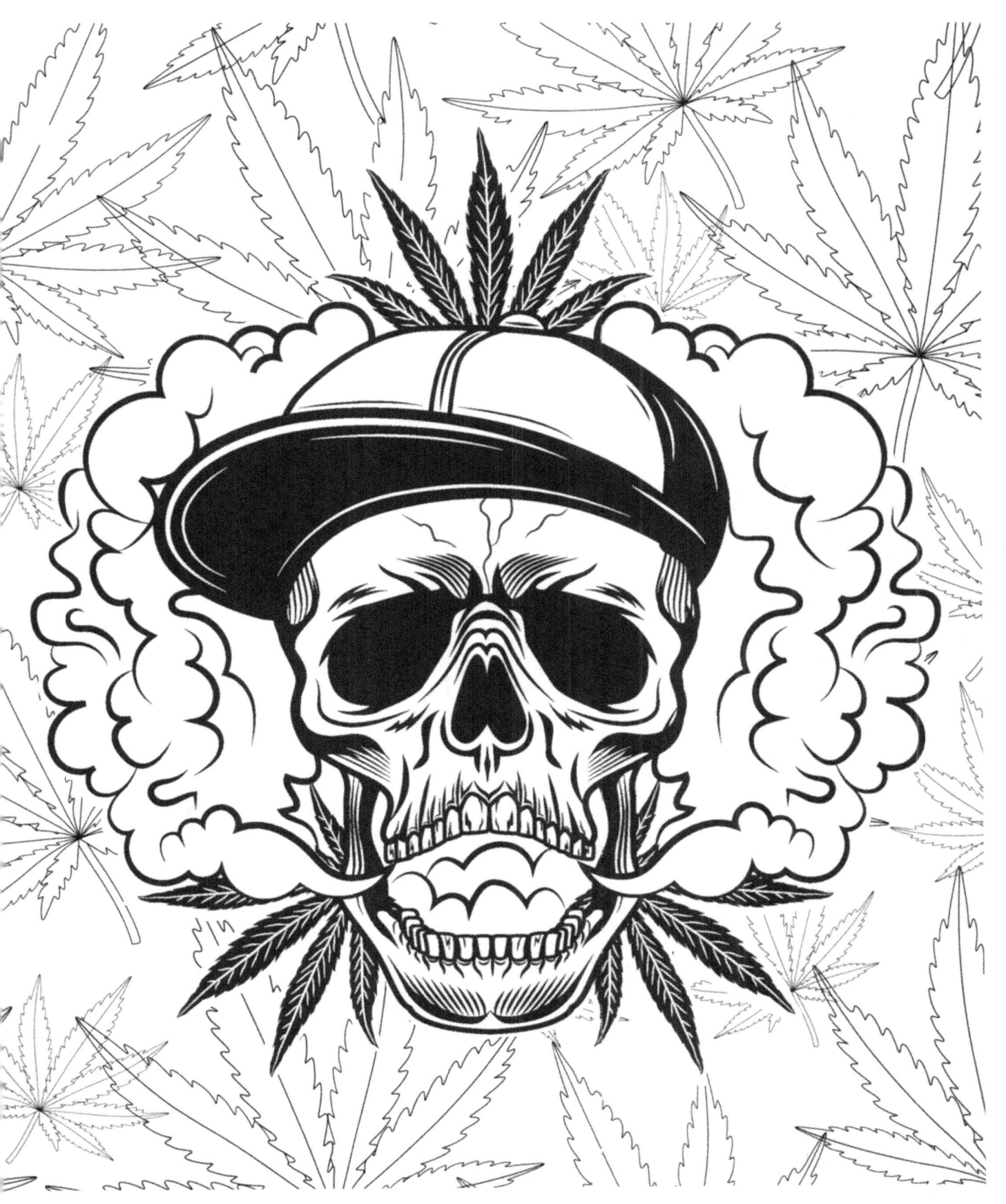

Copyright

R.U. Tokin and C.V. Designs

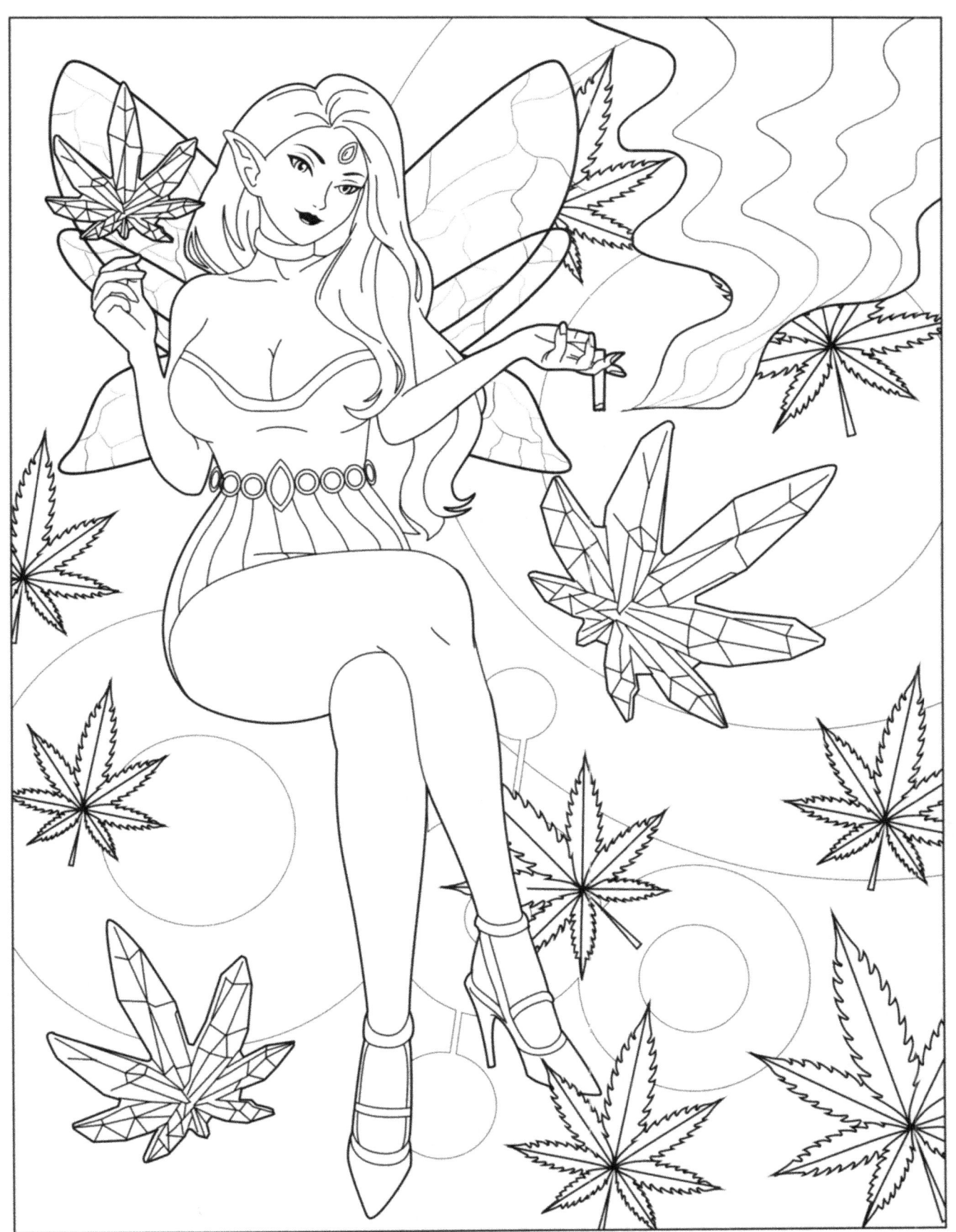

Copyright
R.U. Tokin and C.V. Designs

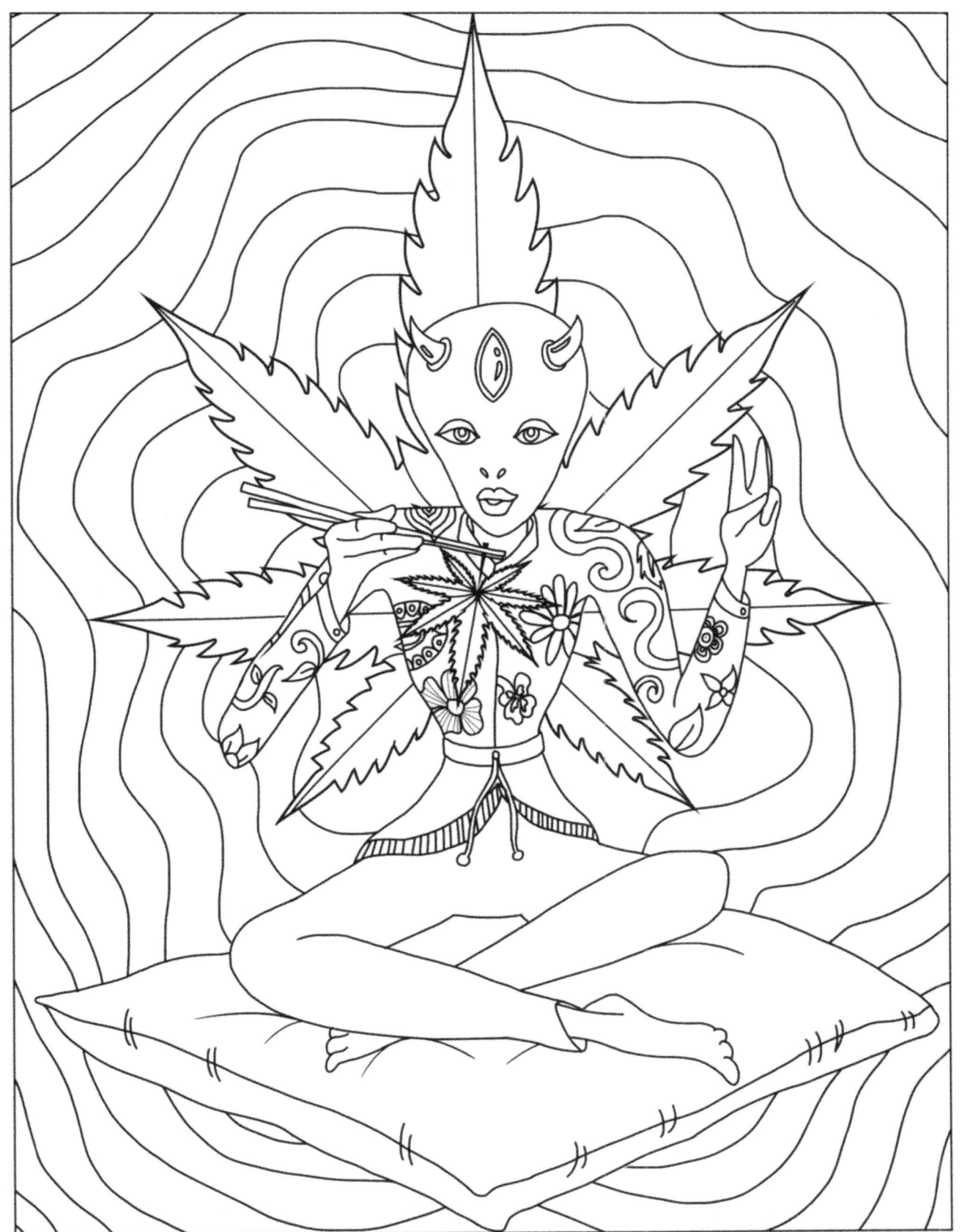

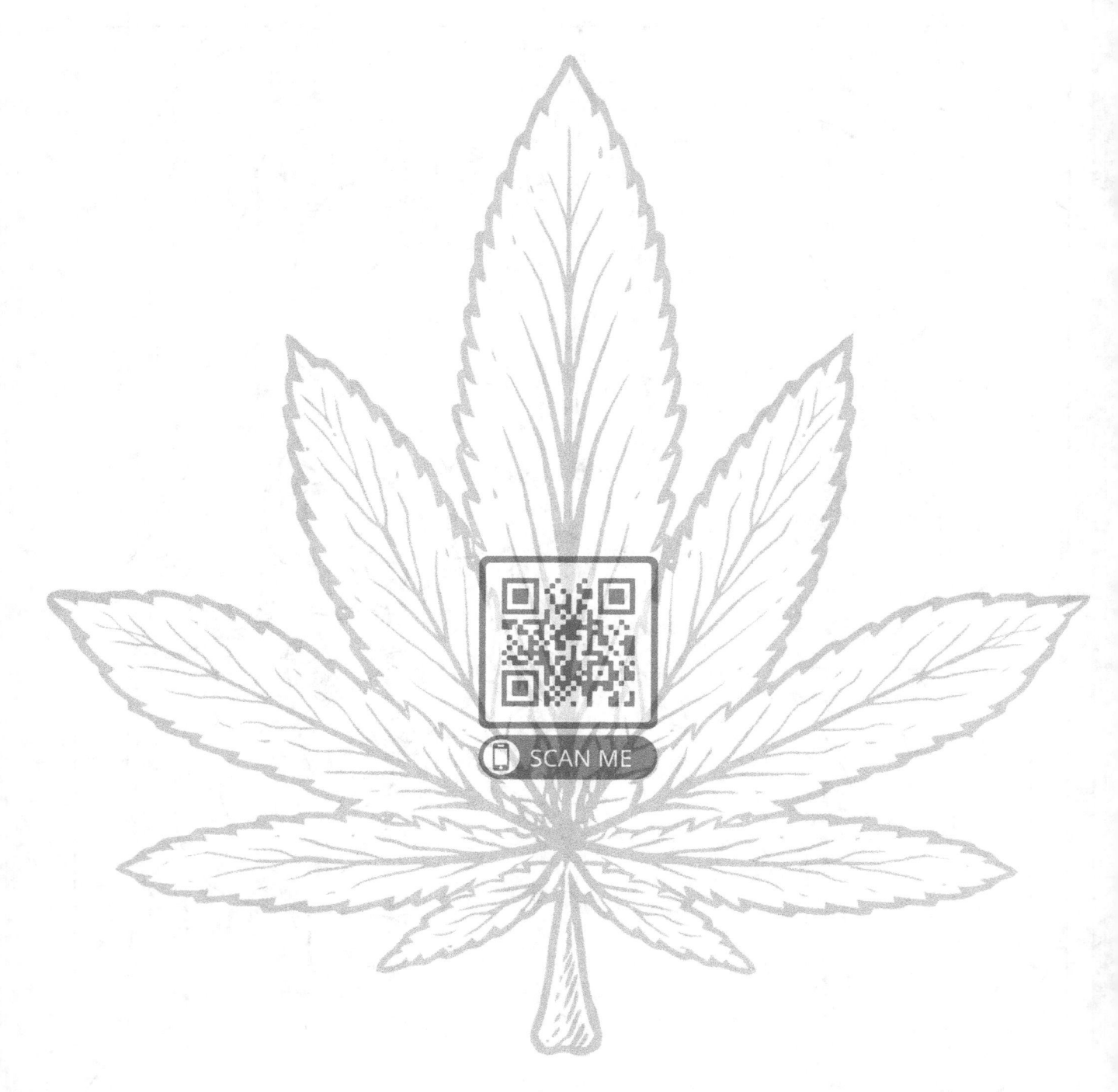

Copyright

R.U. Tokin and C.V. Designs

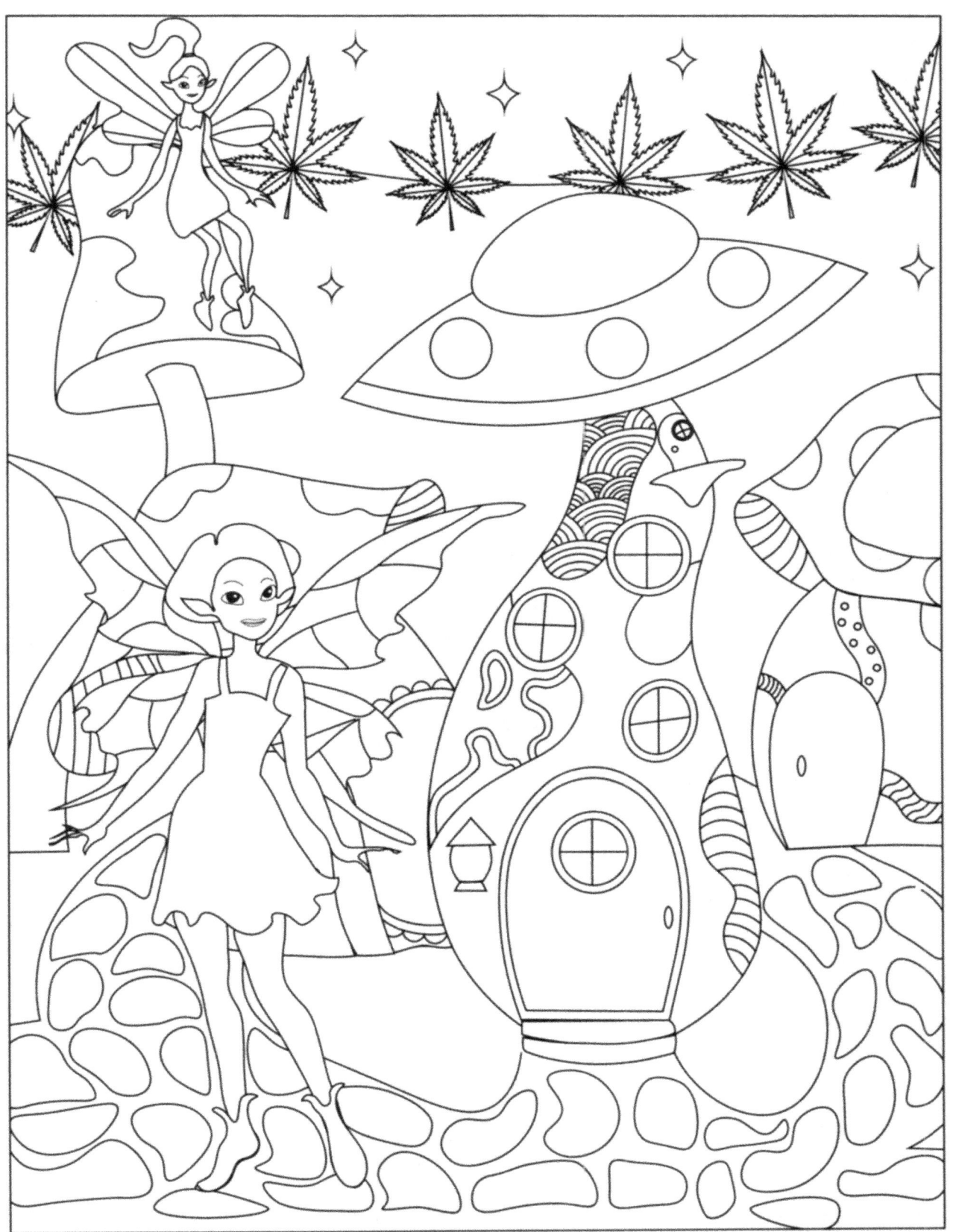

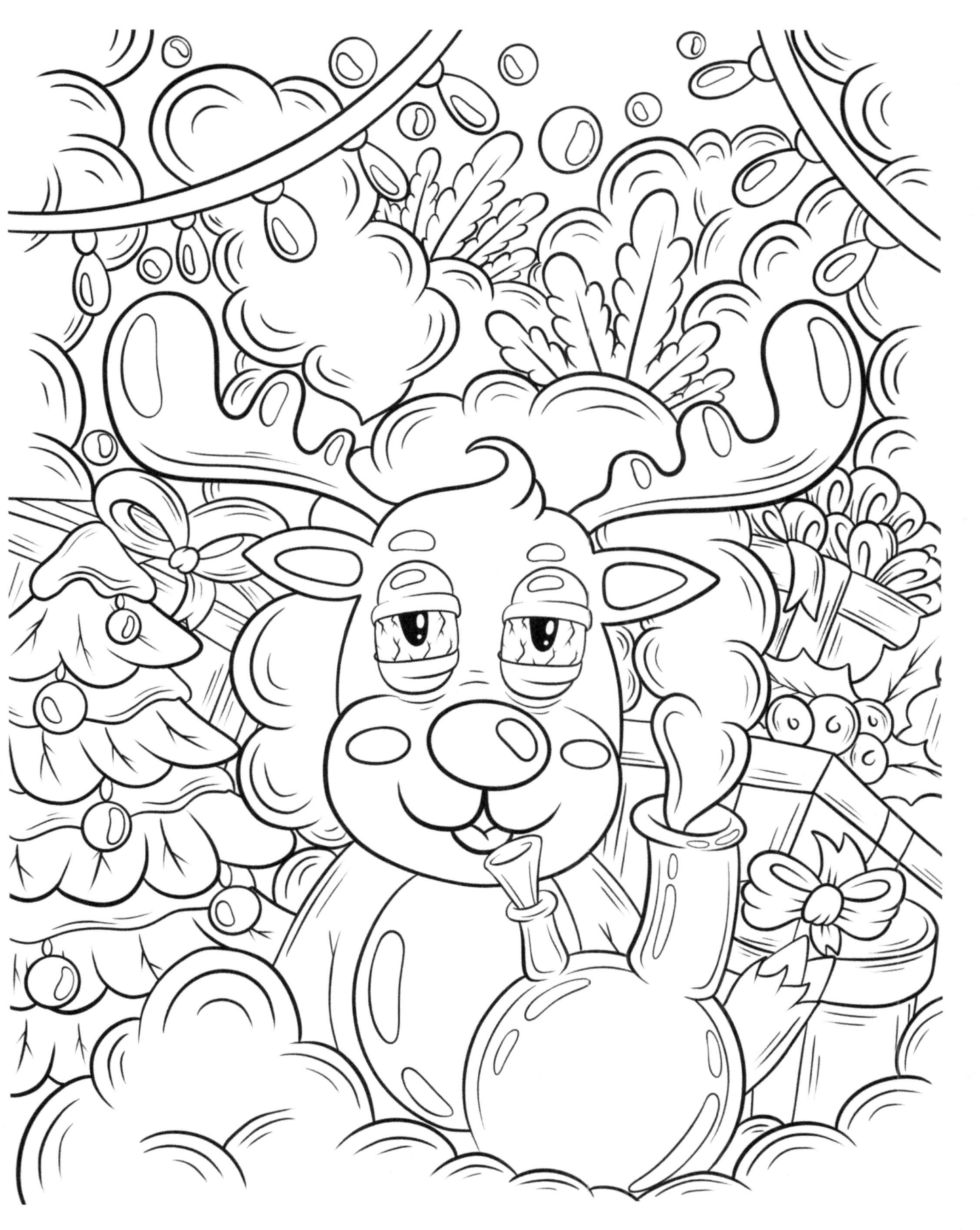

Copyright
R.U. Tokin and C.V. Designs

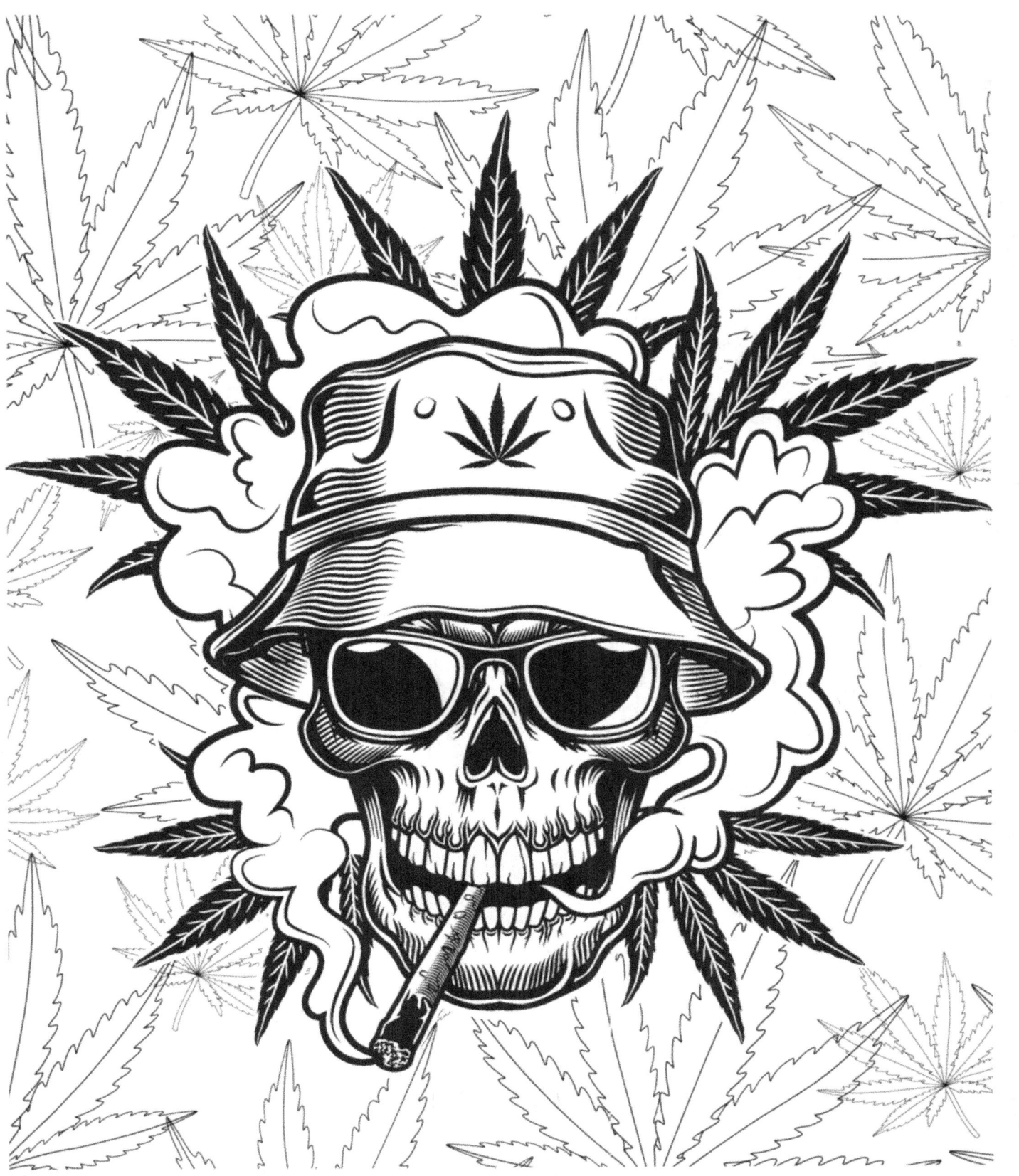

Copyright
R.U. Tokin and C.V. Designs

www.ingramcontent.com/pod-product-compliance
Lightning Source LLC
Chambersburg PA
CBHW060439220526
45465CB00008B/3198